# Fashion Crochet

# Fashion Crochet

## 30 crochet projects inspired by the runway

Claire Montgomerie

CARLTON
BOOKS

THIS IS A CARLTON BOOK

First published in 2012.

This edition published in 2013 by
Carlton Books Limited
20 Mortimer Street
London W1T 3JW

10 9 8 7 6 5 4 3 2

A CIP catalogue record for this book is available from
the British Library.

ISBN 978 1 78097 430 9

Special Photography: Rod Howe
Models: Emily, Elisabeth and
    Scarlett at IMM Models
Stylist: Laia Farran Graves
Hair and Make-up: Emma Turle

Printed in Dubai

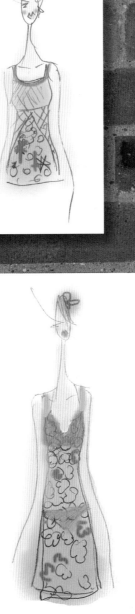

# contents

# INTRODUCTION

Crochet is commonly seen as the poor relative of its sister craft, knitting. It is, erroneously, considered to be impractical for use in clothing (or labelled outdated when it is), with the result that the craft is often relegated to homewares and toys. However with more and more designers championing crochet on the catwalks in recent seasons, I wanted to use their lead to demonstrate how the fabric can be utilized to create fabulously contemporary garments and accessories for the modern woman.

Crochet is being used in many ways on the catwalk and in the high street, by cutting-edge designers such as Marc Jacobs, Henry Holland and Rodarte. The modern fabrics work traditional forms such as granny squares with innovative new stitches and textures. Crochet is incorporated into summery lace and mesh pieces, layered over other garments, worked around the edges of noncrocheted fabrics as an accent, as well as made in bulky yarns as unconventional wintery pieces. All this is a far cry from the traditional ill-fitting crochet of the 1970s, when the craft was most memorably fashionable.

In the early stages of writing this book, I enlisted the talents of some fabulous British crochet designers, who worked with me while I was editor of UK crochet magazine *Inside Crochet*. The main trends from recent seasons were pinpointed and used to inspire a complete on-trend wardrobe. We have provided patterns for all elements of a contemporary wardrobe, from everyday garments to dressy eveningwear and accessories to beachwear. From this innovative collection it should be easy to choose whether to wear crochet from head to toe or simply update a classic outfit by adorning it with a colourful piece of stitched jewellery. I have always considered crochet to be easily adaptable and some of the accessories here are especially simple to modify by changing colour, fibre or quantity to cater for your own taste.

Hopefully this book will provide all the inspiration you need to create wearable, modern, statement pieces to add to your everyday wardrobe, lending a designer air to any outfit with only a tiny price tag.

# PRACTICALITIES

For the purposes of this book, the reader is assumed to have a basic working knowledge of crochet, however, here is a brief summary of some of the most important things to remember. These include tips on yarn, hooks and tension, as the right choice here will enable you to create a beautifully finished and accomplished garment with the least amount of stress.

## TYPES OF YARN

There are countless different types of yarn, including fibre content, weight and construction. Cotton yarn, usually mercerized and very fine, is often considered to be perfect for use in crocheting, as it is strong and smooth; in fact, many people mistakenly think it is the only fibre suitable for this craft. This is most definitely not the case today, as there are many beautiful "knitting" yarns, which are just as fabulous when crocheted. In many cases a single-ply, fluffy, stretchy wool can be easier to work with than the traditional hard cotton. Here is a quick guide to the properties of some of the fibres, which should help you make an informed decision when choosing yarn for a special project.

Whatever fibre you choose, keep a close eye on the construction, as here could lie a pitfall while crocheting. Ensure that the yarn is not too loosely plied, as your hook can slip though the plies, snagging the yarn, while a fancy looped or slubbed yarn may catch in your stitches, making for slow work and untidy stitches.

**Acrylic** Inexpensive, moth resistant and easy to wash, acrylic is a great choice for beginners and creates a smooth working action and neat stitch when crocheting. A mix of acrylic and natural fibres, (such as wool or angora) gives the best drape and handle.

**Alpaca** The fleece from a South American camelid, alpaca is lustrous, silky and very warm, which makes it excellent for hats and scarves. It is, however, very heavy, so be careful when substituting for longer-length garments as it can stretch under the weight.

**Cashmere** Considered the finest of the "noble" fabrics, cashmere is soft, warm, fluffy and expensive. Choosing a cashmere-wool blend will give you many of the benefits of cashmere at a lower cost.

**Cotton** Suitable for open crochet items. Traditionally these would be doilies, but within fashion, cotton is fabulous for summer-weight mesh sweaters and intricate lace items. This plant fibre is readily available and inexpensive; it also has no stretch, which makes for very neat stitching, but can be hard on the fingers.

**Linen** A plant-derived fibre, which can be very rough, this is a great alternative to cotton as it is also strong, with little stretch, making it perfect for accessories.

**Mohair** From the fleece of the angora goat, mohair is soft and seductive, but can be itchy when worn next to the skin. Beware when choosing it for your crochet project, as it is very hard to pick out the individual stitches within a mohair fabric and it can be difficult to unravel, so it may be best to use this fibre only when you are a master of the craft, or for simpler projects.

**Silk** Light, lustrous and shiny, yet very strong, silk is a great choice for summer-weight garments and eveningwear. It is also a fabulous alternative to the traditional crochet staple, cotton, as it is usually single plied, smooth and strong, making it easy to use and neat to work with.

**Wool** There is a vast variety of wool types but all of them are easy to use, warm and elastic and usually give great stitch definition. Merino is the finest and softest sheep's wool. When substituting wool for a traditional cotton fibre, remember that it has more stretch and so will be easier to work with, yet will create a very different type of fabric. Crocheted fabric has little stretch, which makes it perfect for items such as bags as they will be stronger and hold their shape.

## YARN WEIGHTS

Substituting yarn can be one of the most confusing things when following a pattern. If you want to use a different yarn to the one stated in the pattern and do not want to adapt the pattern at all, you must look for a yarn in a similar weight (or thickness) to the one stated, otherwise the fabric will give a different tension and the garment may come out the wrong size. To make matters worse, there are different terms for each category of weight; these differ between manufacturers and sometimes the weights are referred to as "plies". This can be confusing, as a ply refers to how many strands of the fibre are spun together to make the yarn. However, for example, some yarns comprised of two "plies" together result in a sportweight or "4-ply" thickness. It is always best to refer to the ball band for the tension/gauge of the yarn when knitted than to pay too much attention to what the manufacturer has called the yarn. Here is a general guide to the main categories.

**Laceweight/2-ply**  A very fine yarn used mainly to crochet shawls and fine lace patterns. Often this very fine yarn is worked on a slightly larger hook to accentuate the lace pattern.

**Superfine/crochet cotton/3-ply/fingering**  Very thin yarns used for light, detailed and fine work such as doilies and lace. This weight was a popular choice in the past for all kinds of homewares, although today a slightly thicker yarn is more commonly used for speed. Often fine-weight lace patterns can be recreated in much chunkier yarn to give a stunning effect.

**Fine/baby/4-ply/sport**  Used in adult garments to create a fine-gauge, lightweight fabric, perfect for layering and the changing seasons.

**Light/DK/light worsted**  A very standard, practical weight of yarn used commonly in crochet as a lightweight yet quick-to-work choice.

**Medium/Aran/worsted**  A weight of yarn that has become very common, it was traditionally used in Aran sweaters, hence the reference to this weight,

but has become a modern favourite as it is perfect for accessories such as scarves and hats and works up quickly.

**Bulky/chunky**  A thick yarn, used to create chunky fabrics and sweaters, that works up extremely quickly on a larger hook yet is not so bulky that it becomes hard to wear. Not commonly used in the past, this weight has become more widespread as time becomes more of a luxury to modern stitchers.

**Super bulky/roving**  For crocheting on hooks in excess of a 10 mm (N-13) hook.

## CROCHET HOOKS

Hook size is metric in millimetres (mm) in Europe. In the USA, a totally separate system is in use, where either letters or a different numbering system is employed. International magazines and books should give hook size in both mm and in US sizes. You will need all the hooks stated in the pattern if you crochet to the tension the designer has given.

There are many different types of hook, but metal are probably the most common. These are fast to work with, as the yarn slips easily over the shaft, however they do not have any flexibility and can be hard to grip as their shafts are only as large as the hook size, which can be very small if working with fine lace fabric. Hooks with handles, especially padded, shaped or so-called "ergonomic" hooks, can be fabulous at relieving tension in aching hands and much easier to grip. Bamboo and wooden hooks can sometimes snag the yarn, making for slower work, but these often have pretty carved ends, which are popular. Plastic hooks are probably the least slippery and are very light and bendy, which can make them extremely hard to work with, especially with strong, unstretchy yarns.

### Crochet Hook Sizes

| Metric | UK | US |
|--------|----|----|
| .60 mm | | 14 |
| .75 mm | | 12 |
| 1mm | | 11 |
| 1.25 mm | | 7 |
| 1.50 mm | | 6 |
| 1.75 mm | | 5 |
| 2 mm | 14 | B-1 (2.25 mm) |
| 2.5 mm | 12 | C-2 (2.75 mm) |
| 3 mm | 10 | D-3 (3.25 mm) |
| 3.5 mm | 9 | E-4 (3.5 mm) |
| | | F-5 (3.75 mm) |
| 4 mm | 8 | G-6 |
| 4.5 mm | 7 | 7 |
| 5 mm | 6 | H-8 |
| 5.5 mm | 5 | I-9 |
| 6 mm | 4 | J-10 |
| 6.5 mm | 3 | K-10½ |
| 7 mm | 2 | |
| 8 mm | | L-11 |
| 9 mm | | M |
| 10 mm | | N-13 |
| 12 mm | | O/P-15 |
| 15 mm | | Q |
| 20 mm | | S |

### TENSION/GAUGE

A tension swatch is used to ensure you are crocheting at the tension called for in the pattern. It is essential in order to achieve the right size of garment. To do this, you need to crochet a small square of just over 10 cm (4 in) square in the main yarn and stitch used in the pattern, or work a special tension swatch as outlined by the pattern, then count and calculate the average amount of stitches or pattern repeats per cm (in). Work a few more stitches and rows than the tension in the pattern suggests. This way a true gauge is achieved within the square, as the edge stitches can often get distorted. When you have completed the swatch, use a measuring tape or ruler to take some average measurements – count how many stitches and rows to 10 cm (4 in) at different points over the swatch.

Don't worry if your tension is not correct the first time, as crochet is not a precise art and everybody tends to crochet at a different tension; in fact, gauge varies from person to person and also when different stitch combinations, yarn fibres, and hook material are used and when working in the round.

If you find you have more stitches per cm (in) than indicated in the pattern, then your tension is too tight and you need to crochet more loosely. The best way to do this is to increase the size of hook you use by a quarter or half millimetre until the tension is as close as you can get it. If there are fewer stitches than required, then you are too loose, and you need to decrease the size of hook used in the same way.

Once you have the correct amount of stitches per cm, you will find that the garment will work up to the correct size. Of course, crocheting a tension swatch takes time, and with some small projects, where a good fit is not required, such as jewellery, you need not complete a swatch unless you really want to ensure the size.

### JOINING AND FINISHING

The finishing of a garment is often something that crocheters dislike doing, as good finishing is not even noticed when the garment is complete, but bad finishing is glaringly obvious.

When sewing up the crocheted pieces, try to keep the joins as invisible as possible. Always place the pieces next to each other on a flat surface with right sides facing and, if you wish, you may place markers at intervals up the edge to ensure you are sewing up evenly. Use a very neat mattress stitch to connect the edges, or crochet them together using a slipstitch, being sure to use the same colour of yarn as in the main body so that when the seams are pulled and moved when worn, the joining yarn cannot be seen.

Never cut the loose ends of yarn left at the edges of your fabric less than 10–20 cm (4–8 in) long, as these can slip through the loops of the stitches easily and unravel. However, these ends need to be tidied. There are many ways of doing this, for example by threading the ends in and out of the stitches on the reverse side of the work. This can be achieved by hooking through with a small hook, or by darning in and out using a large darning or nitter's needle. You can also crochet over these loose ends as you go, holding the yarn along the top of the last row and catching it in with every stitch you work.

## BLOCKING

It is amazing how much can be achieved to neaten your finished pieces with simple blocking techniques. Crocheted fabrics look more professional once blocked, as the fabric will open up, giving better stitch definition, more even edges and a fabulous drape. You must always block or steam your crocheted garment before you sew it up so that you can ensure all pieces are the correct size and none will buckle. For simple garments, you can get away with simply pinning the pieces to shape and then lightly steaming to set the stitches.

Some crocheted pieces, especially those that need a more stiff, three-dimensional finish, such as some bags and most jewellery, do not need blocking at all. However, with lace and with any piece that has, for some reason, been worked to the wrong measurements, you must block the pieces carefully.

You can buy specialist blocking wires, especially good for large lace pieces such as shawls or scarves. However, you can achieve the same effect by teasing your crochet gently to shape, pinning with blocking or marking pins to your ironing board, or if that is not big enough, a large blanket or towel laid flat on the floor. Once pinned, lay a very slightly damp towel or cloth on top of your fabric and then iron gently. Be careful not to press with the iron as you do not wish to flatten the naturally airy stitches, only to let the heat and steam set the stitches into shape. Once the whole piece is warmed and steamed thoroughly, leave to cool down and dry completely, then you can unpin and remove the piece.

## Abbreviations

Below are the standard abbreviations used for UK crochet patterns. Crochet terminology is different in the US, so below is also the US equivalents to the UK versions.

| UK | | US | |
|---|---|---|---|
| ch | chain(s) | ch | chain(s) |
| dc | double crochet | sc | single crochet |
| dtr | double treble | tr | treble |
| htr | half treble | hdc | half double crochet |
| miss | miss | sk | skip |
| quintr | quintuple treble | trtr | triple treble |
| qtr | quadruple treble | qtr | quadruple treble |
| sl st/ss | slipstitch | sl st/ss | slip stitch |
| tr | treble | dc | double crochet |
| trtr | triple treble | dtr | double treble |
| yrh | yarn round hook | yo | yarn over hook |

| | |
|---|---|
| alt | alternate |
| beg | begin/beginning |
| blk(s) | block(s) |
| ch sp | chain space |
| CC | contrasting colour |
| cont | continue/continuing |
| dec | decrease/decreasing |
| foll | follows/following |
| inc | increase/increasing |
| lp(s) | loop(s) |
| MC | main colour |
| patt(s) | pattern(s) |
| rem | remain/remaining |
| rep | repeat/repeating |
| rnd(s) | round(s) |
| rw(s) | row(s) |
| RS | right side |
| sp(s) | space(s) |
| st(s) | stitch(es) |
| t-ch | turning chain |
| tog | together |
| WS | wrong side |

| | |
|---|---|
| * | Repeat instructions after asterisk or between asterisks as many times as instructed. |
| () | Repeat instructions inside brackets as many times as instructed. |

Blue Beaded Summer Cape

Granny-Square Cowl

Ruffle Scarf

Evening Cape

# wraps & scarves

Fabric-Fringed Scarf

Green Fern Poncho

Chic Beach Cover-Up

# Granny-Square Cowl

Skill Level:
Basic

The basic
double-crochet
granny square
is easy to
learn and is
a great way
to use up
some of your
yarn stash.
A perennial
favourite,
this pattern
can be as
humble as
your granny's
favourite
blanket or
worked into
chic catwalk-
ready designs.

## Granny-Square Cowl

Claire Montgomerie

An easy-peasy pattern using an old classic motif, this cowl is inspired by Paul Smith and Henry Holland's 2011 catwalk collections and it is a great way to utilize the granny square within a modern accessory. The yarns are a mixture of differing weights and fibres, demonstrating how the granny square motif is perfect for using up your leftover and stash yarns, so start digging through your yarn store to find the perfect colour combination! This pattern also includes a handy step-by-step for joining the motifs without sewing up, saving loads of time and yarn in the process, and creating a pretty pattern within the join.

### YARN
You will need 4 or 5 different shades of yarn for the central motifs and black yarn for joining round.

- 1 x 50 g (2 oz) ball each of Sublime baby cashmere merino wool DK, 116 m (126 yds), in shade 158, ladybug; shade 04, gooseberry; shade 159, pansy; and shade 109, duck
- 1 x 50 g (2 oz) ball of Debbie Bliss cashmerino DK, 110 m (120 yds), in shade 037
- 1 x 100 g (4 oz) ball of Malabrigo 100% merino worsted wool, 198 m (215 yds) in black

### NOTIONS
5 mm (size 6) crochet hook

### MEASUREMENTS
One size

The granny square loses its connotations of fustiness with this scarf from Henry Holland's 2011 Autumn/Winter collection. The pieces are constructed from simple squares, stitched together, in a limited palette of alternating red tones with cream, green or blue with white on a black field.

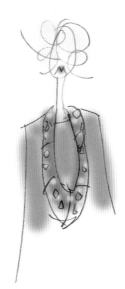

## PATTERN
### Basic Granny Square Motif
Using a 5 mm hook and one of the five central motif yarns, work 6ch. Join with a sl st to form a ring.

**Rnd 1:** 3ch, 2tr in ring, 3ch, * 3tr in ring, 3ch; rep from * 2 more times. Join rnd with sl st to top of first ch. Break off yarn at end of this and every rnd for striped central motif, adding different colours randomly each rnd.

**Rnd 2:** Join new yarn in any ch-3 sp, 3ch, work (2tr, 3ch and 3tr) in same sp, * 1ch, work (3tr, 3ch and 3tr) in next ch-3 sp.
Rep from *2 more times, end with 1ch, join rnd with sl st to top of first ch.

**Rnd 3:** Join yarn in any ch-3 sp, 3ch, work (2tr, 3ch and 3tr) in same sp, 1ch, 3tr in next ch-1 sp, *1ch work (3tr, 3ch and 3tr) in next ch-3 sp for corner, 1ch, 3tr in next ch-1 sp; rep from * around, end 1ch, join rnd with sl st to top of first ch.

Using this simple pattern, you could make as many squares as you wish, as large as you wish, all you would have to do is continue pattern as set, until desired size of granny is achieved, working an extra (1ch, 3tr) in between each corner for every rnd. However, this pattern calls for you to stop at round three for the central motif, then do one more round to join afterwards.

Once you have 18 central motifs, block these lightly and join them with the main, outer edge colour.

### Joining
#### 1st motif, work 4th round complete as follows:
**Rnd 4:** Using 5 mm hook, join main shade yarn in any ch-3 sp, 3ch, work 2tr, 3ch and 3tr in same sp, (1ch, 3tr in next ch-1 sp) twice, *1ch, work 3tr, 3ch and 3tr in next corner sp, (1ch, 3tr in next ch-1 sp) twice. Rep from * around, end 1ch, join rnd with sl st to top of first ch. Fasten off yarn.

Now you will have one finished motif. However, we are not going to finish each motif like this; instead, the next motif is joined along one side to the first motif *as you go*.

#### 2nd motif, work along one side of the square then attach to 1st motif as follows:
**Rnd 4:** Using 5 mm hook, join main shade yarn in any ch-3 sp, 3ch, work 2tr, 3ch and 3tr in same sp, *(1ch, 3tr in next ch-1 sp) twice, 1 ch. Work 3tr, 1ch in next corner sp, now sl st into 2nd of ch3 of any corner ch of first motif, with RS facing, 1ch. Finish off 2nd motif corner with final 3tr in corner sp. Now (sl st into next ch1 sp of motif one, 3tr in next ch-1 sp of motif two) twice, sl st into next ch 1 sp of motif one, 3tr in next 3ch corner sp of motif two, 1ch, sl st into 2nd of ch3

of next corner ch of motif one, 1ch. Finish off 2nd motif corner with final 3tr in corner sp. Now finish off motif 2 edging as a normal granny rnd. (1ch, 3tr in next ch-1 sp) twice, 1ch, work 3tr, 3ch and 3tr in next corner sp, (1ch, 3tr in next ch-1 sp) twice, end 1ch, join rnd with sl st to top of first ch. Fasten off yarn.

Two motifs joined to make one row of the cowl.

**Join 3rd motif to top side of left motif as you joined motifs one and two.**

**4th motif, work along one side of the square then attach to top side of right motif and 3rd motif as follows:**
Rnd 4: Using 5 mm hook, join main shade yarn in any 3ch sp, 3ch, work 2tr, 3ch and 3tr in same sp, * (1ch, 3tr in next ch-1 sp) twice, 1ch. Work 3tr, 1ch in next corner sp, now sl st into 2nd of ch3 of top right corner ch of right motif, with RS facing, 1ch. Finish off 4th motif corner with final 3tr in corner sp. Now (sl st into next ch 1 sp of right motif, 3tr in next ch-1 sp of motif four) twice, sl st into next ch 1 sp of right motif, 3tr in next 3ch corner sp of motif four, 1ch, sl st into 2nd of ch3 of next corner ch of right motif, 1ch. Finish off 4th motif corner with final 3tr in corner sp.

Now attach motif 4 to motif 3 by slip stitching into ch sps along joining sides while finishing last rnd of motif 4 as before, then finish final edge, (1ch, 3tr in next ch-1 sp) twice, end 1ch, join rnd with sl st to top of first ch. Fasten off yarn.

Four motifs are now joined to make two rows of cowl.

Continue to join motifs in this way until 16 motifs have been joined in one long strip, two motifs wide. With the last two motifs, ensure that you join the two ends together into a loop by joining the motifs as you go, joining motifs 1 and 2 to motifs 17 and 18.

## Finishing
Weave in all ends if you have not already done so as you go.

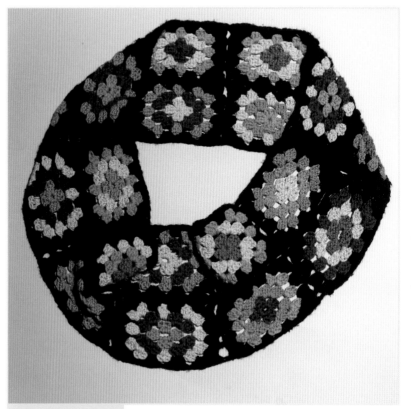

Granny squares can be made of almost any kind of yarn in one colour or many and stitched together to make a scarf. Here, the illusion of colourful central squares stitched into a solid-coloured black field is created by edging each square in black.

# Evening Cape

Skill Level:
Intermediate

With its
sophisticated
ties and
pretty lace
edging,
this cape
would make a
sensational
cover-up over
an evening
dress,
as shown
opposite in
the similarly
delicate
design
by Walter
Rodrigues from
his Autumn/
Winter 2005
collection.

## Evening Cape
Zoë Clements

Capes and ponchos
were fashionable
in the 1970s when
crocheting was a
popular pastime,
so there are many
examples of these
crocheted garments
still around. The
modern versions are
less garish in colour,
and perhaps a little
shorter. Worn most
often as a shoulder-
warmer, they lend
an elegant silhouette
reminiscent of the
Victorian era. This
cape is designed
with a lot of ease
so that bulky winter
coats can be worn
underneath, but the
design looks equally
stunning worn over a
dress as eveningwear.
You can also make
it into a much longer
design, but you will
need additional skeins
of yarn.

## YARN
2 x 100 g (4 oz) skeins of Manos silk blend, 30% silk, 70% merino extrafine wool, 270 m (300 yds) each, in shade 2630, pacific

## NOTIONS
4 mm (size 8) crochet hook
Tapestry needle
150 cm (60 in) purple satin ribbon, approximately 64 cm (2½ in) wide
Sewing needle and matching thread
1 button, 1 cm (½ in) in diameter

## MEASUREMENTS
Bust

| 71–82.5 | 92.5–97.5 | 97.5–102.5 cm |
|---------|-----------|---------------|
| 28–32 | 34–36 | 38–40 in |

Circumference

| 108 | 112 | 118 cm |
|-----|-----|--------|
| 42 | 44 | 46 in |

Length

| 37 | 38 | 39 cm |
|----|----|-------|
| 14.5 | 15 | 15.25 in |

## TENSION/GAUGE
14 rows and 18 sts in Herringbone Hhtr pattern to measure 10 x 10 cm (4 x 4 in).

## SPECIAL INSTRUCTIONS
**Herringbone Half Treble (Hhtr):** *yrh, insert hook in next st, yrh, draw through st and first loop on hook, yrh, draw through both loops on hook.

**Puff Stitch (puff st):** yrh, insert hook into same st as base of 3ch, yrh, pull both loops up to same height as 3ch.

**NOTE:** When working the Flower Mesh, work in rows but do not turn. Keep the same side facing, so that the puff side of the flowers remains on one side. Take time to make sure that the flowers are not twisted before you work into them. This method takes a little practise, as it will feel like you are working backwards.

KEY

· slipstitch

⊙ chain stitch

T Herringbone half treble

◊ puff

## PATTERN

Using 4 mm hook, ch67.

**Row 1:** 1Hhtr in 3rd ch from hook, work into the chains as follows: 1Hhtr, *2Hhtr in next ch, 5Hhtr; rep from * to last 3 sts, Hhtr to end. Turn. *76 sts.*

**Row 2:** ch2 (counts as 1Hhtr now and throughout), 1Hhtr, *2Hhtr in next st, 6Hhtr; rep from * to last 3 sts, 3Hhtr. Turn. *86 sts.*

**Row 3:** ch2, 2Hhtr, *2Hhtr in next st, 7Hhtr; rep from * to last 3 sts, 3Hhtr. Turn. *96 sts.*

### Small Size

**Rows 4–17:** Rep row 3, increasing the number of Hhtr between increases by 1 each row. *196 sts.*

**Next 2 rows:** ch2, Hhtr across. Turn.

**Next row:** ch2, Hhtr2tog, Hhtr to centre, Hhtr2tog, Hhtr to last 3 sts, Hhtr2tog, 1Hhtr. Turn.

**Next row:** ch2, Hhtr across. Turn. *193 sts.*

### Medium Size

**Rows 4–18:** Rep row 3, increasing the number of Hhtr between increases by 1 each row. *206 sts.*

**Next 2 rows:** ch2, Hhtr across. Turn.

**Next row:** ch2, Hhtr2tog, Hhtr to centre, Hhtr3tog, Hhtr to last 3 sts, Hhtr2tog, 1Hhtr. Turn.

**Next row:** ch2, Hhtr across. Turn. *202 sts.*

### Large Size

**Rows 4–19:** Rep row 3, increasing the number of Hhtr between increases by 1 each row. *216 sts.*

**Next row:** ch2, Hhtr across. Turn.

**Next row:** ch2, Hhtr2tog, Hhtr to centre, Hhtr2tog, Hhtr to last 3 sts, Hhtr2tog, 1Hhtr. Turn.

**Next row:** ch2, Hhtr2tog, Hhtr to last 3 sts, Hhtr2tog, 1Hhtr. Turn. Repeat.

**Next row:** ch2, Hhtr across. Turn. *211 sts.*

### Flower Mesh

**Set-up row:** *ch3, puff*, ch3, sl st to base of first 3ch; rep from * to *, miss 2 sts, sl st to next st.

**Set-up row repeat:** ch7, miss 2 sts, sl st to next st, ch3, miss 2 sts, sl st to next st, *3ch, puff*, 3ch, sl st to same st as previous sl st, rep from * to * once more, miss 2 sts, sl st to next st. Repeat across. *Do not turn.*

**Row 1:** ch11, sl st to 4th ch from hook, ch3, work puff in ring just made, sl st to secure, *ch3, sl st to top of centre petal along on foundation row**, ch10, sl st in 4th ch from hook, ch3, work puff st in ring, sl st to 7ch-sp in foundation row, ch3, sl st to ring, ch3, work puff st in ring; rep from * across, finishing the last repeat at **.

**Row 2:** ch9, *sl st in 3ch-sp, ch3, sl st to ring, ch3, work puff st in ring**, ch3, sl st to ring, ch3, work puff st in ring, sl st around 6ch-sp, ch7, sl st to 3ch-sp; rep from * across, ending last rep at **, work a sl st in puff to secure.

**Row 3:** *ch10, sl st in 4th ch from hook, ch3, work puff st in ring, ch3, sl st in ring, ch3, work puff st, sl st to secure**, ch3, sl st to centre petal from last row; rep from *, ending last repeat at **.

**Row 4:** *ch3, sl st in ring, ch3, work puff st in ring, ch3, sl st in ring, ch3, work puff st**, ch7, sl st in next 3ch-sp; rep from * across, ending last repeat at **, sl st to 6ch-sp.

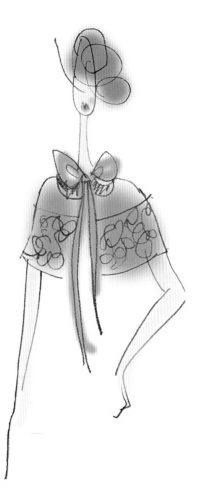

Rep rows 1–4 until fabric is desired length, ending on a row 3. Fasten off.

Re-attach yarn to the last half-flower (made on only 2 petals) along the vertical edge.

Complete the flowers as follows:
ch3, sl st to ring, ch3, work puff st in ring, ch3, sl st to ring, ch3, work puff st in ring, sl st around 7ch-sp**, ch6; rep from * to end, finishing last repeat at **. Fasten off.

### Collar
With WS facing, re-attach yarn to the neck edge.
**Row 1:** ch2, htr(flo) across to centre, 2htr(flo) in centre st, htr(flo) to end. Turn. *66 sts.*
**Row 2:** ch3 (counts as 1tr), 1dc, *1tr, 1dc; rep from * across, working the last dc in the t-ch. Turn.

Repeat row 2 until Collar is desired length, finishing after a WS row. Turn.
*Do not fasten off.*

### Shell Edging
*miss 2 sts, work 5tr in next st, miss 2 sts, sl st to next st; rep from * to end.
Fasten off.

### Finishing
Weave in ends.
Block gently.

Attach button to top of cape section – use the space between the Hhtr as a buttonhole, or create a button loop using a small length of ch.

Cut ribbon in half. Sew each half to the inside top of the cape opening.

Skill Level:
Intermediate

This is a very
delicate take
on the woolly
outerwear cape
by Orla Kiely,
opposite. A
sweet cape
like this
doesn't need
to be worn
only over
dresses; it
can be worn
with a silky
blouse and
jeans for a
more casual
look or over
a lightweight
collarless
coat.

## Blue Beaded Summer Cape

Irina Antonyuk

Continuing the cape trend, this cute little piece is worked in a dense stitch with relief pattern, creating a shoulder adornment ideal for any season. Add beads for a subtle sparkle that's perfect for an evening occasion or sunny summer's day.

## YARN
4 x 50 g (2 oz) balls of Garn Studio cotton viscose,
54% Egyptian cotton, 46% viscose, 110 m
(120 yds) in shade 16, ice blue

## NOTIONS
3.75 mm (size 9) crochet hook
Tapestry needle
Small blue glass beads to decorate
Machine embroidery thread in pale blue

## MEASUREMENTS
Finished cape is 22 cm (9 in) long and 120 cm (47 in)
wide along the lower edge, with 28 cm (11 in) ties.

This pattern is one size, but it's easy to modify should
you want it wider or longer. The overall structure can
be split into 6 sections of 18 stitches plus 1 stitch at
either end (see Fig. 3).

If you want a wider cape, add stitches in multiples of 6.
For a longer cape, repeat Row 19, 6 or more times.

## TENSION/GAUGE
Work the stitch sample to measure around 8 cm (3 in)
by 8 cm (3 in) (see Fig. 1).
**Note:** 3 ch at the start of the row counts as 1 sl st, 1
ch gap between stitches doesn't count as st throughout,
turn work after each row unless otherwise instructed.
Don't worry if the sample comes out a bit bigger than
the measurements. As long as you're happy with the
way it looks, it will work fine as the whole cape.
Make 15dch.

**Row 1:** 3ch, 1tr in first 3t, 1ch, 1tr in next 6 sts, 1 ch,
1 tr in next 5 sts. *15 sts.*

**Row 2:** 3ch, 1tr in next 3sl st, miss next st, puff st into
the 1ch gap, 1ch, puff st into the same gap, miss next
st, 1tr in next 4 sts, miss next st, puff st into the 1ch
gap, 1ch, puff st into the same gap, miss next st, 1tr
into next 3sl st. *15 sts.*

**Row 3:** 3ch, 1tr in next 2 sts, puff st into the gap
between puffs from row below, 1ch, puff st into the
same gap, 1tr in next 4 sts, puff st into the gap, 1ch,
puff st into the same gap, 1tr in next 4 sts. *15 sts.*

**Row 4:** 3ch, 1tr in next 3st, puff st into the 1ch gap,
1ch, puff st into the same gap, 1tr in next 4 sts, puff st
into the 1ch gap, 1ch, puff st into the same gap, 1tr
into next 3 sts. *15 sts.*

**Row 5:** Repeat row 3. *15 sts.*

**Row 6:** Repeat row 4. *15 sts.*

**Row 7:** Repeat row 3. *15 sts.*

**Row 8:** 1ch (doesn't count as st), 1dc in each st along,
including the 1ch gaps. *17sts.*

**Row 9:** 1ch (doesn't count as st), 1blo sl st in each st
along. *17sts.*
Fasten off.

## SPECIAL INSTRUCTIONS
**blo sl st** = back loop only sl stitch.
**blo dc** = back loop only double crochet.

**Double Chain Foundation:** ch 3, insert hook in 1st ch,
pull up 1 loop (2 loops on hook), pull through both
loops, insert into 2nd loop from hook, pull loop through
the 2nd loop (2 loops on hook), pull through both
loops, and so on.

**Puff Stitch (puff st):** yrh, insert hook in stitch, pull up
a loop like with a tr crochet to the height of the row,
yrh, insert hook in same stitch, pull up a loop to the
height of the row again, yrh, insert hook in same stitch,
pull up a 3rd loop the same way – you will have 3
incomplete tr stitches on hook, pull a loop through all
stitches to complete.

Fig. 1
8 cm/3 in

Fig. 3

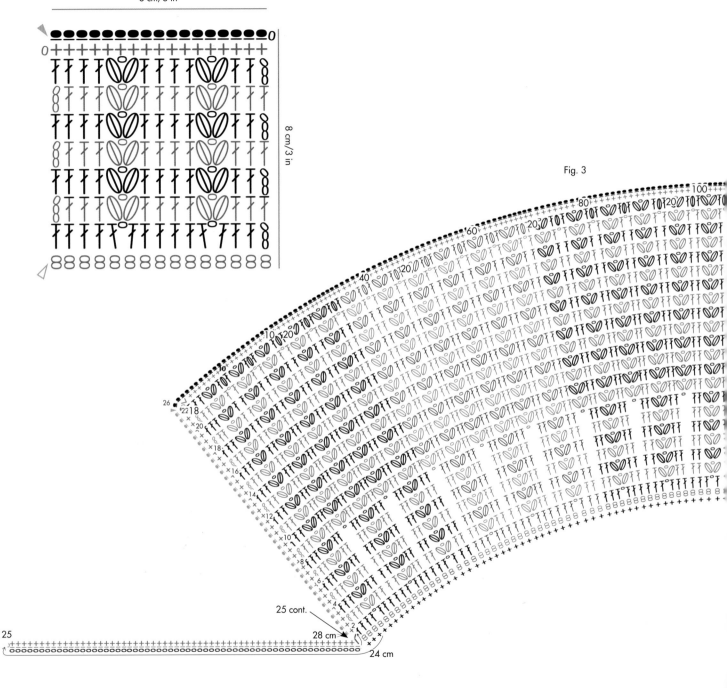

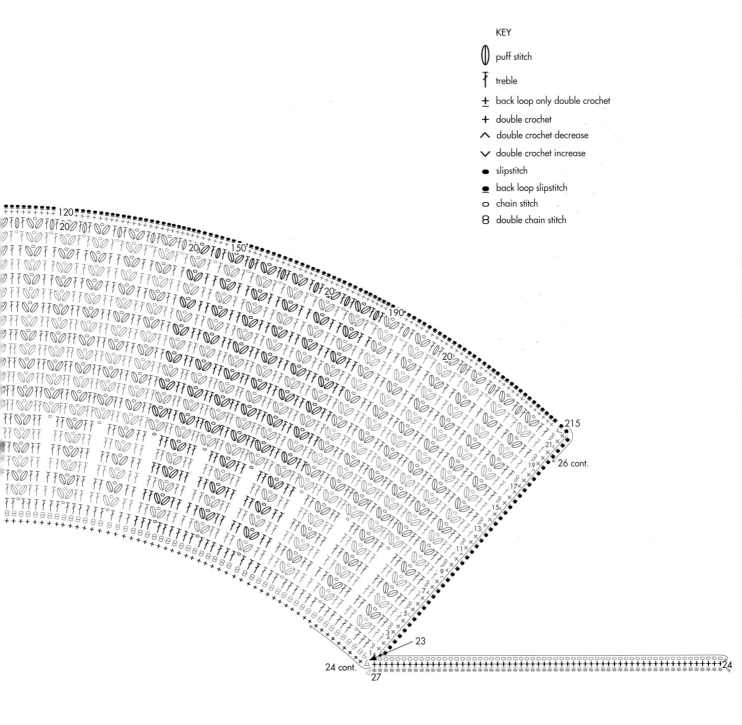

KEY

puff stitch

treble

back loop only double crochet

double crochet

double crochet decrease

double crochet increase

slipstitch

back loop slipstitch

chain stitch

double chain stitch

Fig. 2

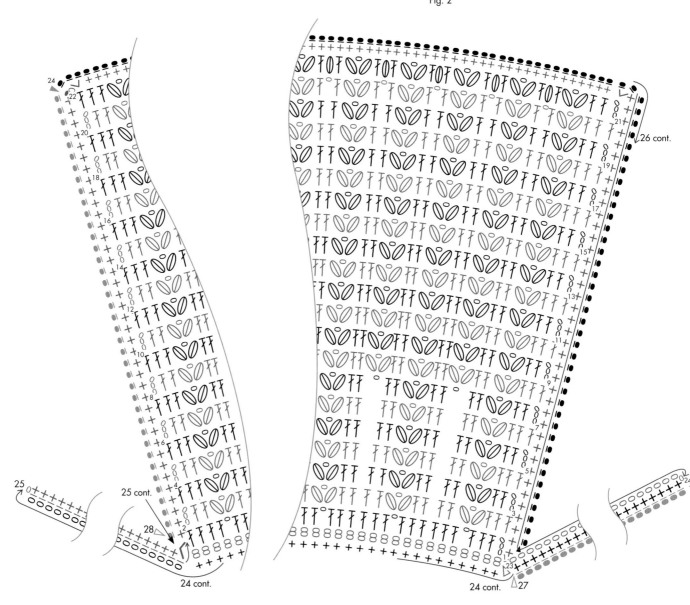

**PATTERN** (see Figs. 2 and 3)
Make 110dch.

**Row 1:** 3ch, 1tr in next 3 sts, 1ch, 17 times (1tr in next 6 sts, 1ch), 1tr in next 4 sts. *110 sts.*

**Row 2:** 3ch, 1tr in next 2 sts, miss next st, 17 times (puff st into the 1ch gap, 1ch, puff st into the same gap, miss next st, 1tr in next 4 st, miss next st), puff st into the last 1ch gap, 1ch, puff st into the same gap, miss next st, 1tr into next 3 sts. *110 sts.*

**Rows 3–6:** Repeat row 2.

**Row 7:** 3ch, 1tr in next 2 sts, 17 times (puff st into the gap between puffs, 1ch, puff st into the same gap, 1tr in next 2 sts, 1ch, 1tr in next 2 sts), puff st into the last gap, 1ch, puff st into the same gap, 1tr in next 3 sts. *110 sts.*

**Row 8:** 3ch, 1tr in next 2 sts, 34 times (puff st into the gap, 1ch, puff st into the same gap, 1tr in next 2 sts), puff st into the last gap, 1ch, puff st into the same gap, 1tr in next 3st. *126 sts.*

**Rows 9–19:** Repeat row 8.

**Row 20:** 3 ch, 1tr in next 2 sts, 34 times (puff st into the gap, 1 ch, puff st into the same gap, 1tr in next st, 1ch, 1tr in next st), puff st into the last gap, 1ch, puff st into the same gap, 1tr in next 3 sts. *126 sts*

**Row 21:** 3ch, 1tr in next 2sts, 34 times (puff st into the gap, 1ch, puff st into the same gap, 1tr in next st, puff st into the 1ch gap, 1tr in next st), puff st into the last gap, 1ch, puff st into the same gap, 1tr in next 3 sts. *178 sts (213 if counting chains).*

**Row 22:** 1ch, 2dc in first st, 1dc in each next st (including 1ch gaps), 2dc in last st, carry on working along the right edge, work 40dc evenly along the edge (allow 2 per row), sl st into the base stitch of row 1. *215 + 40 sts.*

In this project, beads are added as a last step, stitched into the puff stitching to add just a subtle hint of sparkle. Alternatively you might want to use a glitter or pre-beaded yarn to create a more lavishly embellished cape.

**Row 23:** Make 61ch for the tie. *61 ch.*

**Row 24:** Start 2nd ch from hook, 1dc in each st along the tie (60 sts), then carry on working 1dc in ea st along the neck of the cape (110 sts), make 61ch for the other tie. *170 sts + 61 ch.*

**Row 25:** Start 2nd ch from hook, 1 blo dc in each st along the tie (60 sts), dc2tog (foundation ch and base of last st from row 1), work 39dc evenly along the left edge, sl st into the ch at the start of row 22. *120 sts.*

**Row 26:** Carry on from the last sl st, work 1blo sl st into each stitch along the bottom and right edge stop 1 stitch before last. Fasten off. *215 + 39 sts.*

**Row 27:** Attach yarn to the right strap at the 60th dc (before the strap joins the neck of the cape), work 1 blo sl st in ea st. Fasten off. *60 sts.*

**Row 28:** Attach yarn to the left edge at the decreased stitch, work 1blo sl st in each st, fasten off. *39 sts.*

## Finishing

Tidy up any loose ends and stitch on small glass beads individually along the longest puff stitch columns for sparkle.

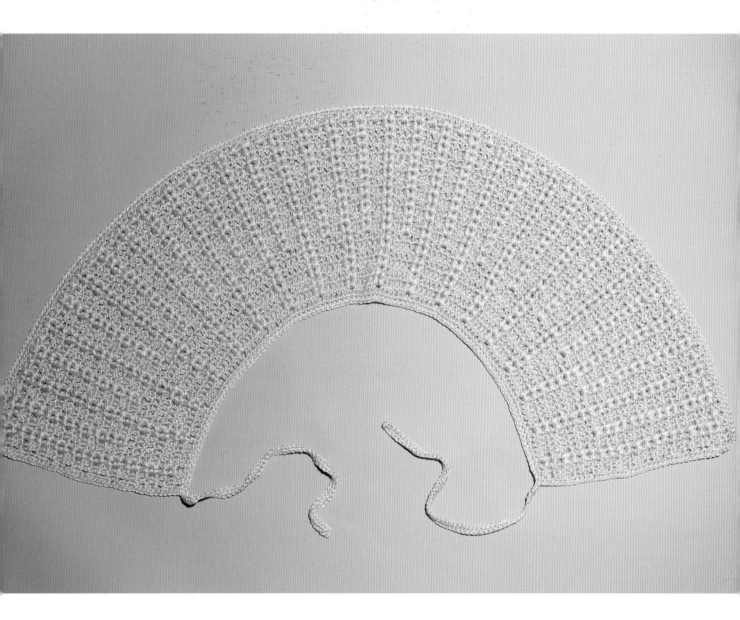

# Ruffle
# Scarf

A high-impact
scarf that
can be worn
several ways,
wrapping
it tightly
around the
neck to form
a "collar"
as here, or
wrapped just
once, worn
as a long,
rolled scarf.

## Ruffle Scarf
Claire Montgomerie

A fabulously extravagant scarf, with as many ruffle rounds as you care to add, this is a really glamorous and colourful yet incredibly warm and practical accessory. It is also easy to adapt it to give more or less fullness – follow the directions where indicated, and don't forget to buy more yarn if you are making it bigger.

The inspiration for this project was a knitted scarf, composed of varying widths and designs of ruffle, that featured in Hussein Chalayan's Autumn/Winter 2011 collection. The British-Turkish Cypriot designer is known for his innovative use of materials as well as for his abstract pieces.

## YARN

1 x 100 g (4 oz) skein of Malabrigo Rios 100% pure merino superwash, 192 m (210 yds) in shade 869, cumparsita (yarn A)

1 x 100g skein of Malabrigo Rios merino worsted, 190 m (205 yds) in shade 503, strawberry fields (yarn B)

1 x 100 g (4 oz) skein of Malabrigo Rios 100% pure merino superwash, 192 m (210 yds) in shade 16, glazed carrot (yarn C)

1 x 100 g (4 oz) skein of Malabrigo Rios 100% pure merino superwash, 192 m (210 yds) in shade 611, ravelry red (yarn D)

## NOTIONS

5.5 mm (size 5) crochet hook
Tapestry needle

## MEAUREMENTS

One size, approximately 150 cm (60 in) in length.

## TENSION/GAUGE

Not necessary for this project.

## SPECIAL INSTRUCTIONS

To make the scarf an alternate length, simply add or subtract a number of chains from the starting chain, ensuring that the overall amount is a multiple of 3.

To add more ruffles, simply add more rows where indicated.

## PATTERN
Using 5.5 mm (size 5) hook and yarn A, ch168.

**Rnd 1:** Working into one side of chain, work 2tr into 3rd ch from hook, *1ch, miss 2ch, work 3tr into next ch*; rep from * to * to last 3ch. *Do not turn.* Miss 2ch, work (3tr, 2ch, 3tr, 2ch, 3tr) all into last ch, then continue along the same length of ch, as before between * and *, along other side of it, working all 3tr groups into the corresponding worked chain. Into last chain work a further 2ch, 3tr, 2ch, join rnd with sl st to top of t-ch.
**Rnd 2:** sl st to next 1ch sp, 3ch, 2tr into same space, *1ch, 3tr into next space *; rep between * and * to first 2ch sp, (3tr, 2ch, 3tr) into next 2ch sp, 1ch, (3tr, 2ch, 3tr) into 2ch sp; rep between * and * to next 2 ch sp, (3tr, 2ch, 3tr) into 2ch sp, 1ch, (3tr, 2ch, 3tr) into next 2ch sp, 1ch, join rnd with sl st to top of first ch.
**Rnd 3:** sl st to next 1ch sp, 3ch, 2tr into same space, *1ch, 3tr into next space *; rep between * and * to first 2ch sp, (3tr, 2ch, 3tr) into next 2ch sp, 1ch, (3tr, 2ch, 3tr) into 2ch sp; rep between * and * to next 2 ch sp, (3tr, 2ch, 3tr) into 2ch sp, (1ch, 3tr into next 1ch sp) to next 2ch sp, (3tr, 2ch, 3tr) into next 2ch sp, (1ch, 3tr into next 1ch sp) to end of rnd, 1ch, join rnd with sl st to top of first ch.

Last round forms base pattern. Rep last rnd once more (or continue working pattern rnd until desired width of scarf is reached). Fasten off yarn A.

Join yarn B to any st of rnd 2, with RS of work facing. 3ch, work 2tr into every st and ch of rnd 2, ignoring stitches from rnd 3. Join rnd with sl st to top of first 3ch. Fasten off yarn B.

Join yarn C to any st of rnd 3, with RS of work facing. 3ch, work 2tr into every st and ch of rnd. Join rnd with sl st to top of first 3ch.
Fasten off yarn C.

Join yarn D to any st of rnd 4, with RS of work facing. 3ch, work 2tr into every st and ch of rnd. Join rnd with sl st to top of first 3ch.
Fasten off yarn D.

Continue in this way for every base pattern rnd you have worked, creating a ruffle on top of the base fabric, at right angles to it for every round.

### Finishing
Weave in all ends and block very lightly – do not press, as the ruffles will flatten.

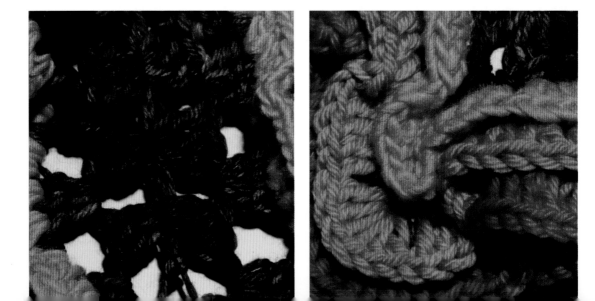

# Fabric-Fringed Scarf

Skill Level:
Basic

The fringing
here is
created by
weaving fabric
lengths into
the scarf
as you work.
We have left
the edges raw
for a looser,
more uneven
effect but
you can use
hemmed strips
of fabric or
ribbon if you
prefer.

## Fabric-Fringed Scarf

Claire Montgomerie

If you experiment with materials other than regular crochet yarns, you can create some spectacular accessories. Here, the fabric strips are crocheted into the fabric as you go, trapping each strand within the stitches to form vertical stripes and a hanging fringe. Try using ribbons if you want to create a crisper fringing.

### YARN
5 x 50 g (2 oz) balls of Sublime baby cashmere merino silk DK, 75% extra fine merino, 20% silk, 5% cashmere, 116 m (127 yds) in shade 006, pebble

### NOTIONS
4 mm (size 8) crochet hook
Fabric cut into 8 lengths of approximately 3 cm (1 in) thick strips, at least 80 cm (31 in) long
Tapestry needle

### MEASUREMENTS
One size, approximately 210 cm (83 in) in length without fringing.

### TENSION/GAUGE
Not necessary for this project.

### SPECIAL INSTRUCTIONS
Where you work dc round the fabric strip to trap the strips, insert hook as with regular dc, yrh, then pull loop through up to height of first turning chain to elongate the regular dc stitch and accommodate the fabric. 2lps on hook, yrh, then finish the stitch as normal by pulling through all loops on hook.

An open-work pattern creates the perfect opportunity to add colour and texture by weaving in ribbon, fabric or yarn. Above a cream scarf and tunic from Bottega Veneta is adorned with orange and red threads, while, opposite, a super-long white crochet scarf by Eley Kishimoto sports a heavy fringe.

This scarf is designed so that the fabric strips begin and end at different points - you can, of course, make them a uniform length. Use pinking shears to cut the fabric if you don't want the edges of the fabric to fray. A multicoloured print will add visual interest to the scarf and break up the colour of the base yarn.

## PATTERN

Using 4 mm (size 8) hook, work a length of chain approx 210 cm (83 in) long, or desired length, ensuring that the amount of chain is a multiple of 2, plus 3.

**Row 1:** Work 1htr into 3rd ch from hook, then 1htr into each ch to end of row.

**Row 2:** (work all dc around a strip of fabric) ch2, hold fabric strip along top of last row, leaving one end hanging at desired length for fringe at start of row, work 2dc, miss 1htr, 1ch, *3dc, 2ch, miss 2htr, (1dc, 2ch, miss 2 htr) twice, 3 dc, 1ch, miss 1htr, (1dc, 1ch, miss 1htr) twice; rep from * twice more, then work in htr, without trapping the fabric strip, to last 60htr. Hold a second length of fabric along top of last row, leaving a section out at the opposite end for the fringe and work all next dc around it. *(miss 1htr, 1ch, 1dc) twice, miss 1htr, 1 ch, 3dc, (miss 2htr, 2ch, 1dc) twice, miss 2htr, 2ch, 3dc; rep from * twice more, 1ch, miss 1htr, 2dc.

**Row 3:** Work straight in htr.

**Row 4:** As row 2, folding back the end of the fabric strip in a "u" shape from last fabric row, and trapping the non-fringe end along the dc parts of the row.

**Row 5:** ch3 (counts as htr, 1ch) *miss next st, htr into next st; rep from * to end of row.

Rows 2–5 form pattern for scarf. Repeat these rows twice more, or for desired width of scarf, but vary the length of fabric you trap into each trapped row. Rep rows 2–4 once more, then work 1 row of htr straight to complete.

### Finishing

Fasten off yarn.
Weave in all ends and block lightly to shape.

# Green Fern Poncho

Skill Level:
Advanced

## Green Fern Poncho

Claire Montgomerie

The classic pineapple stitch is utilized here to produce a stunning, open-lace fabric that provides warmth while creating a lovely contrast against the coloured jumper beneath. Tight and cropped, this poncho is perfect for layering and highlighting the elegant shape of the shoulders. It can even be worn over a lightweight coat.

### YARN
3[4:5] x 50 g (2 oz) skeins of Hipknits handspun cashmere, 110 m (120 yds) in green

### NOTIONS
4.5 mm (size 7) crochet hook
Tapestry needle
Stitch marker

### MEASUREMENTS
Bust

| 76–86 | 96.5–106.5 | 116.5–127 cm |
|-------|------------|--------------|
| 30–34 | 38-42 | 46–50 in |

Length from Shoulder
36 cm
14 in

### TENSION/GAUGE
Neck Ribbing
Work 16 tr and 14 rows to measure 10 x 10 cm (4 x 4 in) using 4.5 mm hook or size required to obtain tension.

Main Body
Patt rep at widest part is approximately 14 cm (5½ in) unstretched.

### SPECIAL INSTRUCTIONS
Double V stitch (DV st): (2tr, 1ch, 2tr) in same st. The poncho is worked entirely in the round, from the neck down, so do not turn work.

Ponchos make a comeback on the catwalk every few seasons. This full-length version from Isabel Marant's Autumn/Winter 2011 collection has a high folded neck for extra warmth that inspired the Green Fern Cowl project.

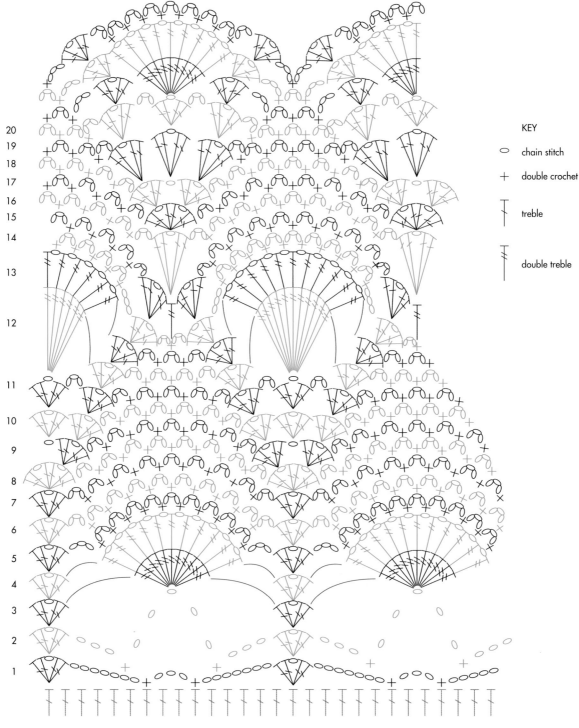

KEY

⬭  chain stitch

+  double crochet

┬  treble

╪  double treble

## PATTERN
### Neck
ch60, sl st into 1ˢᵗ ch to join into a ring.

**Rnd 1:** 3ch (counts as first treble), work 1tr into each chain to end, join rnd with sl st to top of t-ch. *60 sts.*

**Rnd 2:** 3ch (counts as first tr), RtrF, (RtrB, RtrF) to end of rnd, join rnd with sl st to top of t-ch.

Rep rnd 2 until neck measures approx 9 cm (3½ in). Increase rnd: 3ch, work in regular trebles, increasing 30[45:60] sts evenly across rnd, join with sl st to top of t-ch. *90[105:120] sts.*

### Body
**Rnd 1:** 3ch, 1tr into bottom of ch, *7ch, miss 5 sts, 1dc into next st, 3ch, miss 2 sts, 1dc into next st, 7ch, miss 5 dc**, DV st into next st*, rep from * to *, ending last rep at **, work (2tr, 1ch) into bottom of t-ch, join with sl st to top of t-ch. *6 patt reps.*

**Rnd 2:** 3ch, 1tr into bottom of ch, *3ch, 1dc into 7ch arch, 5ch, miss 3ch, 1dc into next 7ch arch, 3ch**, DV st into 1ch sp of DV st*, rep from * to *, ending last rep at **, work (2tr, 1ch) into bottom of t-ch, join with sl st to top of t-ch.

**Rnd 3:** 3ch, 1tr into bottom of ch, *miss 3 ch, work 11dtr into next 5ch arch, miss 3 ch**, DV st into 1ch sp of DV st* rep from * to *, ending last rep at **, work (2tr, 1ch) into bottom of t-ch, join with sl st to top of t-ch.

**Rnd 4:** 3ch, 1tr into bottom of ch, *work (1dtr, 1ch) into each of next 10 dtr, 1dtr into next st**, DV st into 1ch sp of DV st*, rep from * to *, ending last rep at **, work (2tr, 1ch) into bottom of t-ch, join with sl st to top of t-ch.

**Rnd 5:** 3ch, 1tr into bottom of ch, *(3ch, 1dc into 1ch sp) 10 times, 3ch**, DV st into 1ch sp of DV st*, rep from * to *, ending last rep at **, work (2tr, 1ch) into bottom of t-ch, join with sl st to top of t-ch.

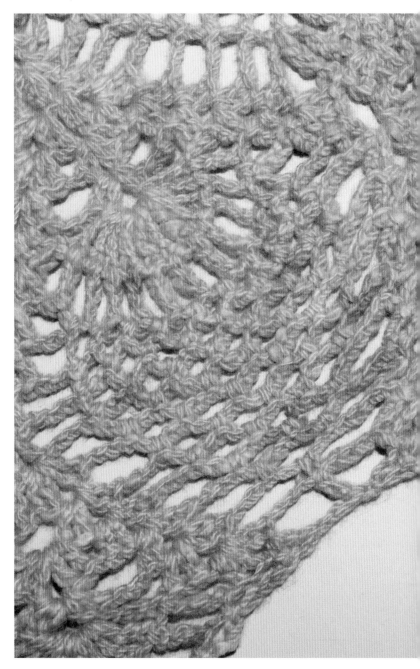

**Rnd 6:** 3ch, 1tr into bottom of same ch, *miss 3 ch, (3ch, 1dc into next 3ch sp) 9 times, 3ch, miss 3 ch**, DV st into 1ch sp of DV st*, rep from * to *, ending last rep at **, work (2tr, 1ch) into bottom of t-ch, join with sl st to top of t-ch.

**Rnd 7:** 3ch, 1tr into bottom of same ch, *miss 3 ch, (3ch, 1dc into next 3ch sp) 8 times, 3ch**, DV st into 1ch sp of DV st*, rep from * to *, ending last rep at **, work (2tr, 1ch) into bottom of first ch, join with sl st to top of t-ch.

**Rnd 8:** 3ch, 1tr into bottom of same ch, *miss 3 ch, (3ch, 1dc into next 3ch sp) 7 times, 3ch, **(2tr, 1ch, 2tr, 1ch, 2tr) all into 1ch sp of DV st*, rep from * to *, ending last rep at **, work (2tr, 1ch) twice into bottom of t-ch, join with sl st to top of t-ch.

**Rnd 9:** 3ch, (1tr, 1ch, 2tr) into bottom of same ch, *miss 3 ch, (3ch, 1dc into next 3ch sp) 6 times, 3ch, ** DV st into next 1 ch sp, 1ch, DV st into next 1 ch sp*, rep from * to *, ending last rep at **, work DV st into next 1ch sp, 1ch, join with sl st to top of t-ch.

**Rnd 10:** 3ch, 1tr into bottom of same ch, DV st into next 1ch sp, *miss 3 ch, (3ch, 1dc into next 3ch sp) 5 times, 3ch, ** work a DV st, into each of next 3 1ch sps*, rep from * to *, ending last rep at **, work DV st into next 1ch sp, (2tr, 1ch) into bottom of t-ch, join with sl st to top of t-ch.

**Rnd 11:** sl st to next 1ch sp, 3ch, (1tr, 1ch, 2tr) into same 1ch sp, 3ch, DV st into 1ch sp of DV st, 3ch, * miss 3 ch, (1dc into next 3ch sp, 3ch) 4 times, **(DV st into 1ch sp of next DV st, 3ch) 3 times*, rep from * to *, ending last rep at **, 3ch, DV st into 1ch sp of next DV st, 3ch, DV st into 1ch sp of next DV st, 3ch, join with sl st to top of t-ch.

**Rnd 12:** sl st to next 1ch sp, 3ch, (1tr, 1ch, 2tr) into same 1ch sp, *(3ch, 1dc into 3ch sp) 3 times, 3ch, DV st into 1ch sp of next DV st, 11dtr into 1ch sp of next DV st, ** DV st into 1ch sp of next DV st*, rep from * to *, ending last rep at **, join with sl st to top of t-ch.

**Rnd 13:** sl st to next 1ch sp, 3ch, (1tr, 1ch, 2tr) into same 1ch sp, *miss 3 ch, (3ch, 1dc into next 3ch sp) twice, 3ch, DV st into 1ch sp of next DV st, (1dtr, 1ch) into each of next 10 dtr, 1dtr into next dtr, ** DV st into 1ch sp of next DV st*, rep from * to *, ending last rep at **, join with sl st to top of t-ch.

**Rnd 14:** sl st to next 1ch sp, 3ch, (1tr, 1ch, 2tr) into same 1ch sp, *3ch, 1dc into 3ch sp, 3ch, DV st into 1ch sp of next DV st, (3ch, 1dc into 1ch sp) 10 times, 3ch**, DV st into 1ch sp of DV st*, rep from * to *, ending last rep at **, join with sl st to top of t-ch.

**Rnd 15:** sl st to next 1ch sp, 3ch, (1tr, 1ch, 2tr) into same 1ch sp, *miss 3 ch, dtr into dc, miss 3 ch, DV st into 1ch sp of next DV st, miss 3 ch, (3ch, 1dc into next 3ch sp) 9 times, 3ch**, DV st into 1ch sp of next DV st*, rep from * to *, ending last rep at **, join with sl st to top of t-ch.

**Rnd 16:** sl st to next 1ch sp, 3ch, 1tr into same 1ch sp, miss dtr, *1ch, 2tr into 1ch sp of next DV st, miss 3 ch, (3ch, 1dc into next 3ch sp) 8 times, 3ch, **2tr into 1ch sp of next DV st*, rep from * to *, ending last rep at **, join with sl st to top of t-ch.

**Rnd 17:** sl st to next 1ch sp, 3ch, (1tr, 1ch, 2tr) into same 1ch sp, *miss 3 ch, (3ch, 1dc into next 3ch sp) 7 times, 3ch**, DV st into next 1ch sp*, rep from * to *, ending last rep at **, join with sl st to top of t-ch.

**Rnd 18:** sl st to next 1ch sp, 3ch, (1tr, 1ch, 2tr, 1ch, 2tr) into same 1ch sp, *miss 3 ch, (3ch, 1dc into next 3ch sp) 6 times, 3ch, **(2tr, 1ch, 2tr, 1ch, 2tr) into 1ch sp of next DV st*, rep from * to *, ending last rep at **, join with sl st to top of t-ch.

**Rnd 19:** sl st to next 1ch sp, 3ch, (1tr, 1ch, 2tr) into same 1ch sp, 1ch, DV st into next 1ch sp, *miss 3 ch, (3ch, 1dc into next 3ch sp) 5 times, 3ch**, 1DV st into next 1ch sp, 1ch, DV st into next 1ch sp*, rep from * to *, ending last rep at **, join with sl st to top of t-ch.

**Rnd 20:** sl st to next 1ch sp, 3ch, (1tr, 1ch, 2tr) into same 1ch sp, DV st into next 1ch sp, DV st into 1ch sp of next DV st, *miss 3 ch, (3ch, 1dc into next 3ch sp) 4 times, 3ch**, (1 DV st into next 1ch sp) three times*, rep from * to *, ending last rep at **, join with sl st to top of t-ch.

**Rnd 21:** sl st to next 1ch sp, 3ch, (1tr, 1ch, 2tr) into same 1ch sp, (3ch, 1DV st into 1ch sp of next DV st) twice, *miss 3 ch, (3ch, 1dc into next 3ch sp) 3 times, 3ch**, (1DV st into next 1ch sp, 3ch) twice, 1DV st into next 1ch sp*, rep from * to *, ending last rep at **, join with sl st to top of t-ch.

**Rnd 22:** sl st to next 1ch sp, 3ch, (1tr, 1ch, 2tr) into same 1ch sp, *9dtr into 1ch sp of next DV st, 1DV st into 1ch sp of next DV st, * miss 3 ch, (3ch, 1dc into next 3ch sp) twice, 3ch**, DV st into 1ch sp of next DV st*, rep from * to *, ending last rep at **, join with sl st to top of t-ch.

**Rnd 23:** sl st to next 1ch sp, 3ch, (1tr, 1ch, 2tr) into same 1ch sp, *(1dtr, 1ch into next dtr) 8 times, 1dtr into next dtr, 1DV st into 1ch sp of next DV st, 3ch, miss 3 ch, 1dc into next 3ch, 3ch**, 1DV st into 1ch sp of next DV st*, rep from * to *, ending last rep at **, join with sl st to top of t-ch.

**Rnd 24:** sl st to next 1ch sp, 3ch, 1tr into same 1ch sp, *(3ch, 1dc into next 1ch sp) 8 times, 3ch, 2tr into 1ch sp of next DV st, miss 3 ch, 1dtr into dc, miss 3 ch**, 2tr into 1ch sp of next DV st*, rep from * to * ending last rep at **, join with sl st to top of t-ch.
Fasten off.

**Finishing**
Weave in ends.
Block lightly to shape.

# Chic Beach Cover-Up

Skill Level:
Intermediate

Ideal for the
beach, this
crocheted
cover-up is
great for
wearing over
your bikini.
On the
catwalk, far
right, is
a "fishermen's
net" style
by Julien
MacDonald,
while opposite
a shawl
version is
worn over a
silver lamé
swimsuit by
Paco Rabanne.

## Chic Beach Cover-Up

Helda Panagery

Poolside style has never been so chic with this fabulously functional beach cover-up, the perfect companion for a bikini or a pair of shorts and a vest. An optional belt adds further options for those who prefer to wear it closed to emphasize the waistline. Made in organic white cotton, it is lightweight and absorbent to keep you nice and cool.

## YARN
6 x 50 g (2 oz) balls of Twilleys Freedom Sincere DK, 100% organic cotton, 115 m (125 yds) in shade 600, snowdrop

### Belt (optional)
40 g (1.4 oz) same yarn

## NOTIONS
6 mm (size 4) crochet hook
4 stitch markers

## MEASUREMENTS
Total width

| 84 | 88 | 90 | 114 cm |
|---|---|---|---|
| 33 | 34½ | 35½ | 45 in |

Right/Left Front to Armhole

| 23 | 24 | 28 | 32 cm |
|---|---|---|---|
| 8½ | 9½ | 11 | 12½ in |

Total Length
79 cm
31 in

## TENSION/GAUGE
Work 6 rows of pattern repeat to 6.5 cm (2.5 in).

## PATTERN NOTES
This top is simply a rectangle, which makes it easily adaptable based on three of your measurements:
1 Left front edge to armhole and the right front edge to armhole (count as one measurement as they will be the same length)
2 Armhole to armhole (back)
3 Desired length.

The beauty of this pattern is you decide whether you want it to skim the body or prefer a looser style. The top is made sideways, allowing it to be tailor-made to fit. The pattern is a 6-row repeat. These 6 rows measure 6.5 cm (2.5 in). You simply keep adding more sets of 6 rows for the fit you like, measuring the top against your body as you go. If you prefer a longer line simply add stitches in multiples of 5. Alternatively, try the top on as you go and simply add more rows for a wider back, left front and right front, or more chains for a longer length.

**NOTE:** Every row has 2 patterns. Placing a marker at the start of next pattern will be a visual aid to remind you to change pattern.

## SPECIAL INSTRUCTIONS
**blo** = back loop only.
**flo** = front loop only.

### Ribbing Pattern 1

These 6 rows are repeated throughout.

**Row 1:** 1 row of htr to end.

**Row 2:** 2ch, turn, 1dc in the next 2htr, *5ch, skip 3htr, 1dc in the next 2 htr**. Repeat from * to ** to marker. Ribbing stitch flo. 1htr in the 22 sts of rib.

**Row 3:** 3ch, turn (acts as a 1tr). 1tr in the back loop of the 22 rib stitches. 1tr in the next 2 htr.* 4ch skip 5ch on the previous row, 1tr in next two htr.** Repeat from *to **.

**Row 4:** 2ch, turn, 1htr in st, *ch2, sl st rows, 2, 3, and this row together, Ch2. 1htr in the next two**. Repeat from * to**. Work flo in the next 22 sts.

**Row 5:** 2ch, turn, work rib blo for 22 sts, PM *4ch, skip stitches from previous row, 1htr in the next two stitches**. Repeat 2ch. Turn.

**Row 6:** htr to end.

### Ribbing Pattern 2

**Row 1 blo:** 1htr in the back loop in every st.

**Row 2 flo:** 1htr in the front loop to end.

Alternate these two rows throughout the garment.

### PATTERN
### Left Front

ch90 place a stitch maker in stitch 22. These are going to be used as ribbing stitches.

**Row 1:** 2ch, turn, 1htr in every htr.

**Row 2:** 2ch, turn, 1htr in every htr to end.

**Row 3:** Repeat row 1.

**Row 4:** Repeat row 1.

**Row 5:** Repeat row 1. (These five rows are the button band).

**Row 6:** 2ch, turn. Do row 2 of pattern 2 until stitch marker, work row 1 of ribbing pattern. I recommend you move the marker on every row it gives you a visual reminder that you are starting rib pattern.

**Row 7:** 2ch, turn. Work row 3 of pattern 1.

**Row 8:** 2ch, turn. Work row 4 of pattern 1.

**Row 9:** 2ch, turn. Work row 5 of pattern 1.

**Row 10:** 2ch, turn. Work row 1.

Continue the 6-row pattern for a further 18 rows, this is for the smallest size. You are making left front to armhole. If you want larger sizes, these 6 rows measure 5 cm (2 in). Repeat these 6 rows until you are happy with the width from your left front to your armhole.

### Armhole Opening

**Row 26:** You should start on row 6 of pattern 1 (armhole should start on the patterned end, not at ribbing end). 1htr in next two stitches, skip the next 32 sts, Place stitch marker. 1htr in every stitch to second marker for ribbing. Rib to end. This opening should measure 20 cm (8 in). If you want a larger opening, skip as many as you like for the fit you like.

**Row 27:** 2ch, turn, rib until stitch marker, lhtr in all stitches including the 32sts of armhole opening that you skipped. Row 1 of pattern 2.

**Row 28:** 2ch, turn, row 2, to st marker, rib to end.

### Back Section, Armhole to Armhole

Continue in pattern until row 67, or until you are at row 6 of pattern 2. Repeat opening as for rows 26 and 27. This measures 33 cm (13 in). For larger sizes increase in sets of 6 rows. 6 rows measure 5 cm (2 in).

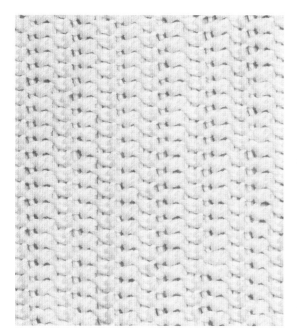

### Right Front

Work a further 24 rows, making sure to use both patterns 1 and 2 on every row.

### Border

Remove stitch markers, 2ch, turn, 1 row htr to end. Do this in the ribbed section. Work a further 4 rows of htr in every htr to end.

### Armhole Border

Holding piece with right side facing ,join yarn at underarm and work 1 row htrs around, adjusting stitches as needed to keep it flat. Join with a sl st to the first htr at start.

Finish off and weave in ends. Repeat for other armhole.

### Neckline Edging

**Row 1:** With right side facing, make 1htr in every st to end.
**Row 2:** 2ch, turn, skip 1htr, 1htr in next st, 2htrtog, 1hdc to last 3 sts, 1htrtog, 1htr in next
**Row 3:** 2ch, turn, 1htr in next st ,2htrtog ,1htr to last 2sts, 2htrtog .
**Row 4:** 2ch, turn, rep row 3. Fasten off weave in ends.

The neckline will have slight decrease at both ends. It is deliberately larger than normal to maintain the rectangular shape. No shaping required.

### Belt (optional)

**Row 1:** ch232. 1htr in third ch from hook, 1htr in every st to end.
**Row 2:** 2ch, turn, 1htr in every htr to end.

Repeat row 2 for a further 4 rows. Fasten off and weave in ends.

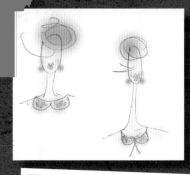

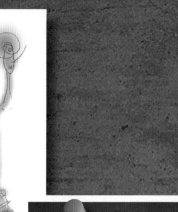

Lace Collar

Mohair Flower Necklace

Crochet Bangles

Ruffle Chain Necklaces

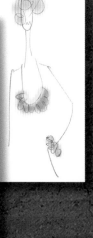

Floral Corsages

accessories

Cloche Hat

Bobble Bag

Straw-Inspired Tote

Chain Shoulder Bag

## Lace Collar

Claire Montgomerie

A very sweet recent trend is for lace collars that embellish the necklines of all kinds of outfits. Some are trims on preppy sweaters, blouses and dresses, while others are accessories in their own right, to be worn as a pretty adornment. This intricate lace collar can be worn either way, sewn to the neckline of a crew-neck sweater or tied round the neck of any outfit to instantly update it.

Skill Level: Basic

The girlish high-neck lace collar from Erdem Moralioglu, left, was a natural pick to inspire the delicate crocheted collar with ribbon, opposite. Known for his floral prints and lacy layering, the designer creates ultra-feminine fashions.

## YARN

1 x 50 g (2 oz) ball of Malabrigo Lace, 100% merino wool, 430 m (470 yds) in shade 09, polar morn

## NOTIONS

2 mm (size 14) crochet hook
162 cm (64 in) length of 5 mm (¼ in) wide ribbon
Tapestry needle

## MEASUREMENTS

Collar measures approximately 40 cm (16 in) around inside edge

## TENSION/GAUGE

Not necessary for this pattern.

## PATTERN

Using 2 mm (size 14) hook, ch 121.
**Row 1:** Work 1dc into 2nd ch from hook, then 1dc into each ch to end of row. Turn. *120 sts.*
**Row 2:** ch3, tr into next st, ch1, *miss next st, 4tr, ch1; rep from * to last 3 sts, miss next st, 2tr. Turn.
**Row 3:** 2ch, 8htr, 2htr into next st, (9htr, 2htr into next st) to end of row. Turn. *132 sts.*
**Row 4:** 11htr, 3ch, miss 2sts, (25htr, 3ch, miss 2sts) 4 times, 11htr. Turn.
**Row 5:** *dc to next ch sp, 5tr into ch sp; rep from * 4 more times, dc to end of row. Turn.
**Row 6:** dc to next tr, *(5ch, dc into next tr) 4 times, 5ch, 12dc, 3dc into next st, 12dc; rep from * 3 further times, (5ch, dc into next tr) 4 times, 5ch, dc into next dc, dc to end of row. Turn.
**Row 7:** 10dc, *5ch, miss next st, (dc into ch sp, 5ch) 5 times, miss next dc, 25dc; rep from * 3 further times, 5ch, miss next st, (dc into ch sp, 5ch) 5 times, miss next dc, dc to end of row. Turn.
**Row 8:** dc to one st before next ch sp, *5ch, miss next st, (dc into ch sp, 5ch) 6 times, miss next st, dc into next st. Turn and (work 7dc into next ch sp, sl st into dc) 7 times, dc into next st. Turn, (5ch, dc into centre dc of next 7dc group) 7 times, 5ch, miss 3dc of dc group and next dc, dc into next st, dc to one st before next

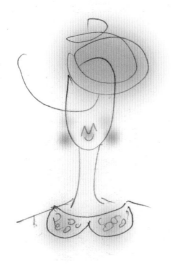

5ch; rep from * three further times, 5ch, miss next st, (dc into ch sp, 5ch) 6 times, miss next st, dc into next st. Turn and (work 7dc into next ch sp, sl st into dc) 7 times, dc into next st. Turn, (5ch, dc into centre dc of next 7dc group) 7 times, 5ch, miss 3dc of dc group and next dc, dc into next st, dc to end of row. Turn.

**Row 9:** dc to one st before next ch sp, *5ch, miss next st, (dc into ch sp, 5ch) 8 times. Turn, and (work 7dc into next ch sp, sl st into dc) 9 times, dc into next st. Turn, (5ch, dc into centre dc of next 7dc group) 8 times, 5ch, miss 3dc of dc group and next dc, dc into next st, dc to one st before next 5ch; rep from * three further times, 5ch, miss next st, (dc into ch sp, 5ch) 8 times, miss next st, dc into next st. Turn and (work 7dc into next ch sp, sl st into dc) 9 times, dc into next st. Turn, (5ch, dc into centre dc of next 7dc group) 9 times, 5ch, miss 3dc of dc group and next dc, dc into next st, dc to end of row. Turn.

**Row 10:** dc to one st before next ch sp, *5ch, miss next st, (dc into ch sp, 5ch) 10 times, miss next st, 15dc; rep from * 3 further times, 5ch, miss next st, (dc into ch sp, 5ch) 10 times, miss next dc, dc to end of row. Turn.

**Row 11:** dc to ch sp, sl st into bottom of first ch, *(work 7dc into next ch sp, sl st into next dc) 11 times, dc to next ch sp; rep from * to end of row. Turn.

**Row 12:** *(5ch, dc into centre dc of next 7dc group) 11 times, 5ch, miss one dc, dc into next st; rep from * four further times, ending with last dc into last st of row. Turn.

**Row 13:** (6ch, dc into ch sp) 12 times, *3ch, miss next dc, dc into next ch sp on next scallop, (6ch, dc into ch sp) 11 times; rep from * twice more, *3ch, miss next dc, dc into next ch sp on next scallop, (6ch, dc into ch sp) 12 times, dc into last st of row. Turn.

**Row 14:** 1ch, (9dc into next ch sp, sl st into dc) 11 times, *1ch, miss next ch sp, 1dtr into 3ch sp, 1ch, (9dc into next ch sp, sl st into dc) 9 times; rep from * twice more, 1ch, miss next ch sp, 1dtr into 3ch sp, 1ch, (9dc into next ch sp, sl st into dc) 11 times. Turn.

**Row 15:** (7ch, dc into centre dc of next 9dc group) 11 times, *5ch, dc into dtr, 5ch, dc into centre dc of next 9dc group, (7ch, dc into centre dc of next 9dc group) 8 times; rep from * twice more, 5ch, dc into dtr, 5ch,

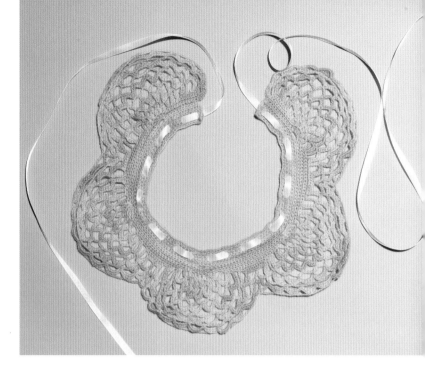

dc into centre dc of next 9dc group, (7ch, dc into centre dc of next 9dc group) 10 times, 7ch, dc into last st of row. Fasten off yarn.

## Finishing
Weave in all ends and block lightly to shape. Thread ribbon in and out of holes in neck edge and tie in a bow to fasten.

# Ruffle Chain Necklaces

Skill Level:
Basic

## Ruffle Chain Necklaces

Claire Montgomerie

The simple crochet ruffle makes a fabulous edging or trim to garments but can also be utilized on its own as stunning jewellery when added to gold chains. Layer up the ruffles in different colours and stripes for a striking statement piece, which is young and modern. Here, the neon shades are perfect for an on-trend summer accessory. Necklaces can easily be made longer, shorter, thicker, thinner, more or less layered and ruffled more tightly or softly (see pattern notes for details). Alternatively, sew a simple, small ruffle to a short chain for an understated bracelet.

### MATERIALS
1 x 50 g (2 oz) ball each of Rico Essentials Merino DK, 100% soft merino wool, 120 m (131 yds) in shade 64, electric lime (yarn A); shade 73, bright orange (yarn B); shade 71, lobster (yarn C); shade 04, acacia pink (yarn D)

### NOTIONS
4 mm (size 8) crochet hook
Large-link gold-coloured metal chains in varying lengths
Tapestry needle

### TENSION
Not necessary for this project.

### MEASUREMENTS
Layered short ruffle necklace: 64 cm (25 in), circumference with the ruffle 25 cm (9¾ in) long.

**Single ruffle necklace:** 78 cm (30 in) circumference, with inside (lobster shade) ruffle of 35 cm (13¾ in) and outer (orange shade) ruffle of 45 cm (17¾ in).

**Bracelet:** 22 cm (8¾ in) circumference.

Daydream Nation, formed of design duo Jing and Kay Wong, created a range of crochet necklaces for Peter Jensen's "Laurie" collection using crocheted pieces, chains and oversized pearls. This version, the Grande Chrysanthemum, has a deeply frilled collar that is easy to re-create in different colours, widths and lengths.

## PATTERN NOTES

Below are the exact patterns for each accessory, however you will begin to see that you can easily adapt each pattern to suit your own taste. For longer/shorter ruffles, simply make your foundation chain longer or shorter accordingly.

For thicker or thinner ruffles, add or subtract rows or use longer or shorter stitches (trebles for long rows, dc for short) or a mixture of stitches.

For more tightly ruffled pieces, work more increase rows, or increase more quickly, up to 3 or 4 stitches into every stitch when increasing.

For more softly ruffled pieces, work less increase rows, or increase less quickly – every other row or every third row, or work increases into every other stitch instead of every stitch.

Play with the ruffles and have fun!!!

## LAYERED MULTICOLOURED RUFFLE NECKLACE

Using 4 mm (size 8) hook and yarn C, work a length of chain as long as desired ruffle; in this case the chain was approx 25 cm (9¾ in) long.

### First Layer
**Row 1:** Work 1 dc into 2nd ch from hook, then 1dc into each ch to end. Turn.
**Row 2:** 1ch, work 2dc into each dc to end of row. Turn.
**Row 3:** 1ch, work 1dc into each st to end of row. Turn.
**Row 4:** 1ch, work 2dc into each dc to end of row. Turn. Fasten off yarn A.

### Second Layer
Attach yarn B into foundation chain of first layer.
**Row 1:** Work 1dc into each chain of first layer foundation chain. Turn.
**Row 2:** 1ch, work 2dc into each dc to end of row. Turn.
**Row 3:** 1ch, work 1dc into each st to end of row. Turn.
**Row 4:** 3ch, work 2tr into each st to end of row. Turn.

**Row 5:** 1ch, 1dc into each st to end of row. Turn. Change to yarn C.

**Row 6:** 1ch, work 2dc into each dc to end of row. Turn. Fasten off yarn C.

### Third Layer
Attach yarn D to back of row 1 of 2nd layer.
**Row 1:** Working into back of each st of row 1, work 1dc into each st to end of row. Turn.
**Row 2:** 1ch, work 2dc into each dc to end of row. Turn.
**Row 3:** 3ch, 1tr into each st to end of row. Turn
**Row 4:** 3ch, work 2tr into each st to end of row. Turn.
Rep last 2 rows once more. Fasten off yarn D.

## SINGLE RUFFLE NECKLACE IN ORANGE

Using a 4 mm (size 8) hook and yarn B, work a length of chain as long as the desired ruffle; in this case the chain was 45 cm (17¾ in) long.

**Row 1:** Work 1 dc into 2nd ch from hook, then 1dc into each ch to end.
**Row 2:** 1ch, work 2dc into each dc to end of row.

The layered multicoloured necklace, right, uses three differently coloured lengths worked in tiers, but for something a bit simpler, make several single-coloured necklaces, as opposite, and wear them stacked together.

**Row 3:** 1ch, work 1dc into each st to end of row.
**Rows 4 and 5:** 1ch, work 2dc into each dc to end of row.
**Row 6:** 1ch, work 1dc into each st to end of row. Fasten off yarn.

## SINGLE SOFT RUFFLE NECKLACE IN LOBSTER

Using 4 mm (size 8) hook and yarn C, work a length of chain as long as desired ruffle; in this case the chain was 35 cm (13¾ in) long.

**Row 1:** Work 1 dc into 2nd ch from hook, then 1dc into each ch to end.
**Row 2:** 1ch, work 2dc into each dc to end of row.
**Row 3:** 1ch, work 1dc into each st to end of row.
**Row 4:** 1ch, work 2dc into each dc to end of row.
**Row 5:** 1ch, work 1dc into each st to end of row.
**Row 6:** 1ch, (work 2dc into next st, 1dc) across row. Fasten off yarn.

## BRACELET

Using 4 mm (size 8) hook and yarn C, work a length of chain as long as desired ruffle; in this case the chain was
22 cm (8¾ in) long.

**Row 1:** Work 1 dc into 2nd ch from hook, then 1dc into each ch to end.
**Row 2:** 1ch, work 2dc into each dc to end of row.
Work last round 4 further times. Fasten off yarn.

## Finishing

Finish all necklaces/bracelets in the same way.

Take desired length of chain and, if long enough to slip over the head or hand easily, join into a ring. If not, attach a jewellery clasp to both ends of the chain.

Sew the foundation chain of the ruffle securely to the centre front of the metal chain, using matching yarn and tapestry needle. Weave in all ends neatly.

Do not block ruffles as they will stand prouder without blocking.

## Mohair Flower Necklace

Claire Montgomerie

A statement necklace is an easy way to inject colour and fun into any wardrobe. These floral motif necklaces can be layered up or worn alone and are bold and colourful yet delicate and pretty enough to be worn in many ways, teamed with anything from a feminine tea dress to a bold, colour-block, high-fashion T-shirt.

The basic flower shape can be adapted – try differing sizes of chain lengths for petals in the second round to make a pansy, or add more petals for a daisy. You can also work a further round, padding out each petal with double crochet stitch in the same way that you covered the first yarn ring.

Skill Level:
Basic

Heaping multiple strands of crocheted garlands can create a beautiful effect, transforming a simple accessory into the focal point of an outfit as shown here by a model wearing a dress by A Colecionadora at the Autumn/ Winter 2005 collection at Rio Fashion Week in Brazil.

## YARN
1 x 25g (1 oz) ball of Rowan Kidsilk Haze, or equivalent mohair-blend yarn, 210 m (229 yds) in any colour

## NOTIONS
4–4.5 mm (size 8–7) crochet hook
Darning needle

## MEASUREMENTS
Necklace measures approx 50 cm (19½ in) all round for the 12 flower long necklaces shown, but you can make the necklaces as long as you wish.

## TENSION/GAUGE
Not necessary for this project but each flower should measure approximately 4cm (1½ in) in diameter.

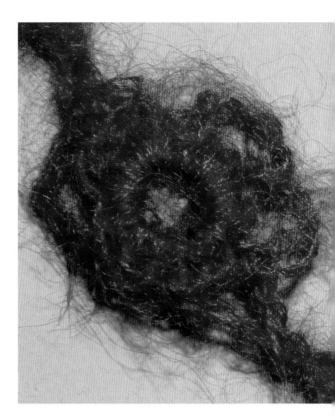

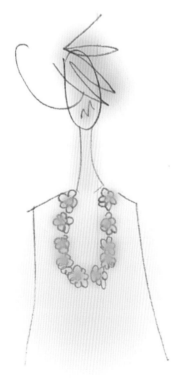

## PATTERN
### Basic Flower
Wrap yarn round a finger (or a chunky crochet hook) 8 or 9 times. Remove the loop from your finger and hold so that the yarn is kept in a secure ring.

**Rnd 1:** Work 1dc into the ring, holding the loop securely so that the yarn does not unravel. Work a further 17dc into the ring. sl st to first dc to join rnd.

**Rnd 2:** 5ch, (miss 2dc, dc into next st, 5ch) to end of rnd, sl st into bottom of first 5ch.
Fasten off yarn.
Weave in end to central loop.

### Second Flower

Now work a 2nd flower to last petal of rnd 2.

**Last petal:** 2ch, sl st into 3rd ch of any petal of first flower, 2ch, finish off rnd as usual.

Fasten off yarn.

Weave in end to central loop.

### All Following Flowers

Work next flower to last petal of rnd 2.

**Last petal:** 2ch, sl st into 3rd ch of 3rd petal of previous flower, 2ch, finish off rnd as usual.

Fasten off yarn.

Weave in end to central loop.

### Last Flower

Work last flower to 3rd petal of rnd 2.

**Third petal:** 2ch, sl st into 3rd ch of 3rd petal of previous flower, 2ch, finish off petal as established, work to 6th petal.

**Sixth petal:** 2ch, sl st into petal opposite joined petal of first flower, 2ch, finish off rnd as usual.

Fasten off yarn.

Weave in end to central loop.

# Crochet Bangles

Skill Level:
Basic

## Crochet Bangles
Claire Montgomerie

Bangles have been big news for many seasons, with a common trend to pile them high on one or both arms, using bracelets of differing widths, textures and colours. Make one or two of these and wear them singly or with your regular bangles for a splash of colour and a contrast in texture. Alternatively make lots in different widths and colours and wear them all at once for an up-to-the-minute fashion statement.

### YARN
1 x 50 g (2 oz) ball (using small amounts only) of Sirdar Snuggly Baby Bamboo DK, 80% bamboo sourced viscose, 20% wool, 95 m (104 yds) in shade 159, jack in the box (yarn A); shade 162, toy box red (yarn B); shade 160, paintbox pink (yarn C); shade 132, putty (yarn D); shade 161, baby berries (yarn E); shade 123, yummy yellow (yarn F)

### NOTIONS
3.5 mm (size 9) crochet hook
Assorted plastic bangles to fit your arm
Tapestry needle

### MEASUREMENTS
Assorted sizes, widths of bangles as desired. Pictured bangles are approximately 4 cm (1½ in), 2 cm (¾ in) and 1 cm (½ in) in width.

### TENSION/GAUGE
Not necessary for this project.

The design of the bracelets above, on the catwalk of Donna Karan's Spring/Summer 2011 collection, inspired the crocheted embellishment worked over plastic bangles of varying sizes, opposite.

The medium-sized crochet design, above, needs a wider bangle base to display the more open stitches, whereas the "bobble row" effect on the bracelet opposite works well on very thin bangles too as the base is entirely wrapped with the yarn.

## WIDE BANGLE PATTERN

For the wider, 4 cm (1½ in) bangle pictured, using 3.5 mm (size 9) hook and yarn A, work 23ch (if you want to work a wider or smaller bracelet, ensure your starting chain is a multiple of 4, plus 3).

**Row 1:** 1tr into 7th ch from hook, *3ch, miss 3ch, 1tr into next ch; rep from * to end of row.
**Row 2:** 2ch, *2ch, 1dc in 2nd ch of next ch sp, 2ch, 1tr into next tr; rep from * to end of row.
**Row 3:** 5ch, 1tr into next tr, *3ch, 1tr into next tr; rep from * to end of row.

Repeat rows 2 and 3 until piece is long enough to go round the entire circumference of bangle.

Join two short ends of piece into a round using a sl st join. Fasten off yarn and block piece to shape.

Insert bangle into fabric loop and sew up the long seam of the piece around the inside of bangle. Weave in ends.

## MEDIUM BANGLE PATTERN

For the 2 cm (¾ in) bangles pictured, using 3.5 mm (size 9) hook and yarns B or C, work 10ch (if you want to work a wider or smaller bracelet, ensure your starting chain is an even number).

**Row 1:** Work 1dc into 2nd ch from hook, then work 1dc into each ch to end of row. *9dc.*
**Row 2:** ch1, work 1 row of dc straight.
**Row 3:** ch4 (counts as 1tr, 1ch), *miss 1dc, work 1tr into next st, 1ch; rep from * to end of row.
Work 2 rows straight in dc.

Repeat last 3 rows until piece is long enough to go round the entire circumference of bangle.

Join two short ends of piece into a round using a sl st join. Fasten off yarn and block piece to shape.

Insert the bangle into fabric loop and sew up the long seam of the piece around the inside of bangle. Weave in ends.

## NARROW BANGLE PATTERN
For the 1 cm (½ in) width of bangle pictured, using 3.5 mm hook (size 9) and yarns D, E or F, work dc all round it, through the centre, ensuring that you squish as many as you can in to cover the plastic thoroughly. You may need to keep pushing up the dc as you go.

### Bobble Row
*Work a chain of length 3–5ch, sl st into base of ch, sl st across to where you want next bobble; rep from * to end of rnd, fasten off yarn.
Weave in ends.

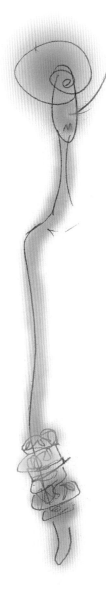

Skill Level:
Basic

Crochet
corsages
strung onto a
leather thong,
right, make a
stunning re-
interpretation
of the
multicoloured
crocheted
scarf at
the Autumn/
Winter 2003
showing of the
Petro Zillia
fashion line,
opposite.
Mixing up
the types of
yarn textures
within a
flower - such
as cotton,
mohair and
alpaca -
adds visual
interest.

## Floral Corsages
Helda Panagary

These beautiful
blooms can be worn
in an infinite amount
of ways. The most
flamboyant display
is to wear them all at
once as on oversized
necklace or in a huge
bouquet corsage.
All the blooms are
finished with a brooch
back, so they can
be worn singly or in
clusters. They can
also be used to adorn
accessories such as
bags, shoes and sun
hats, or made with
a clip backing for
the hair.

## YARN

1 x 50 g (2 oz) ball of DMC Natura Just, 100% combed cotton, 155 m (170 yds) in shade 18, coral (yarn A)

1 x 50 g (2 oz) ball Drops cotton viscose, 54% Egyptian cotton, 46% viscose, 110 m (120 yds) in shade 12, teal (yarn B)

1 x 25 g (1 oz) ball Debbie Bliss Angel, 76% superkid mohair, 24% silk, 200 m (218 yds) in shade 009, baby blue (yarn C)

1 x 50 g (2 oz) BC Garn Silkbloom Fino, 45% mulberry silk, 55% soft merino, 200 m (218 yds) shade 07, green (yarn D)

1 x 50 g (2 oz) Drops alpaca, 100% alpaca, 166 m (182 yds) in shade 7238, lime (yarn E)

## NOTIONS

6 mm (size 4) crochet hook
7 mm (size 2) crochet hook
Brooch backs
Tapestry yarn
Needle and thread
Leather thong (optional)

## TENSION/GAUGE

Not necessary for this project.

## SPECIAL INSTRUCTIONS

Make as many flowers you like, playing with the yarn and hook sizes to create different effects.

**Fasten off invisibly:** Simply break the yarn, leaving an end long enough to sew with, and pull it though the loop of the last stitch. Thread it onto a needle and take the needle under the two strands of the first stitch. Then take it back into the last stitch to form a new stitch, or alternatively pull it tight until it disappears. Fasten off by darning in the yarn end along the chain edge.

**Cluster 1 (Cl1)** = 1tr, 2ch, 1tr
**Cluster 2 (Cl 2)** = 2tr, 2ch, 2tr
**blo** = back loop only.
**flo** = front loop only.

### ROSE PATTERN

Make 2. Using 6 mm (size 4) hook ch50. For a smaller rose, begin with less chains.

**Row 1:** 1tr in 4th chain from hook, 2ch, 1tr in the same ch,* 2ch, skip 2ch, cl1, 2ch, skip 2ch, cl1; rep from * to last ch, 1tr.
**Row 2:** 3ch, turn, *cl2 in 2ch of cl1 from previous row, 2ch, cl2 in 2ch of cl1; rep from * to last st 1tr.
**Row 3:** Turn, make *10tr in cl2 of previous row, 1ch, 1dc in 2ch space of previous row, 1ch; rep from* to last st, 1tr. Fasten off invisibly (see special instructions).

**Making up:** Roll up loosely from the one end to the other, play around with the fabric until you have the flower shape, stitch the bottom edges together to form a flat base along the chain edge. Steam if necessary. Sew the brooch back to the flat side.

### LARGE MULTILAYERED BLOOM PATTERN

Using 6 mm (size 4) hook, begin with an adjustable ring.
**Rnd 1:** ch1, then work 15htr into the ring. Join with sl st in 1st htr. *15 sts.*
**Rnd 2:** ch3 (counts as 1tr), then work 1tr into the same st. Work 2tr into the next st. Work 2tr into each st around. sl st into top of t-ch.
**Rnd 3:** Work in front loops only. Each petal will take 5 sts in total.
Change colour. Insert hook through flo of first st.** ch1, work 1dc into same st, 1htr into next st, 5tr into next st, work 1 htr into next st, then 1dc into next st. dc. Continue working around the circle, sl st into the ch1 you made at the very beginning to close the round.** Fasten off. *6 petals.*
**Rnd 4:** Work in back loops of round 2, using the same colour. You will be working behind the petals you've already made. ch3 (counts as 1tr), work 1tr into same st. Work 1tr into next st, *2tr into next st, 1tr into next st; rep from * all the way round. sl st into 3rd ch of initial ch3 to close the round. *45 sts.* Do not fasten off.
**Rnd 5:** Work in front loops only. Begin by making a sl st into flo of first st. Make your first petal (round 3 from ** to **). Make 8 further petals. *9 petals.*
Fasten off and steam lightly.

The multi-layered bloom and rose, opposite left and right, make beautiful single corsages to pin on a jacket, dress or handbag; alternatively, cluster a few flowers together as a bigger brooch, as seen right.

Chrysanthemum
and peony
corsages,
opposite top
and bottom,
make lovely
adornments for
any outfit.
On the left,
a turquoise
peony was
pinned onto
a ponytail
band to make
a pretty hair
decoration.

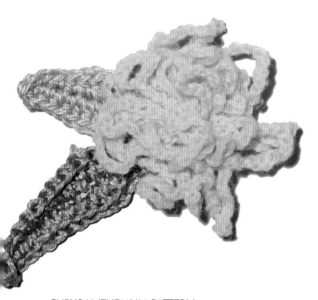

## LEAF PATTERN

Using 7 mm (size 2) hook and one of the green shades (make one of each colour for every flower), ch 14.

sl st in 2nd chain from hook. 1dc in the next 3ch, 1htr in the next 2ch, 1tr in the next 3ch, 2htr in the next 2ch, 1dc in next, 3dc in last ch. Work around the other side of foundation row. 1dc in next ch, 1htr in the next 2ch, 1tr in next 3ch, 1htr in next 2ch, 1dc in next 3ch, slip stitch in next ch.

Fasten off invisibly (see Special Instructions).

### Finishing

For all flowers take a light green leaf and the dark green leaf and play around with the flower until it is pleasing to your eye and it resembles a flower with two petals. Sew them in position, then sew brooch back to the bloom. Fasten and sew in all ends.

## CHRYSANTHEMUM PATTERN

Using 6 mm (size 4) hook:
**Row 1:** 4ch, Miss 2ch, 1dc in each of the next two ch. ch15, turn, 1dc in each of the 2 dc.
**Row 2:** 1ch, turn, 2dc, 15ch, turn, 1dc in each of the next 2 sts.

Repeat row 2 for 30 rows. Fasten off invisibly (see Special Instructions).

Pin out the loops and steam. Roll the straight edge loosely, stitch through the centre a few times to form a flat base. Sew the brooch back to the base.

## PEONY PATTERN

Using 7 mm (size 2) hook, begin with an adjustable ring.

**Row 1:** 15 htr, join with slip st in first htr made. Make 3ch, 2tr all in the same stitch. In every htr make 3tr in each to end. Join with slip st to first tr.
**Row 2:** 3ch. Do not turn. Make 2tr in same place. 3tr in every tr to end. For the small one, fasten off here. For large, repeat row 2. Fasten off and weave in ends.

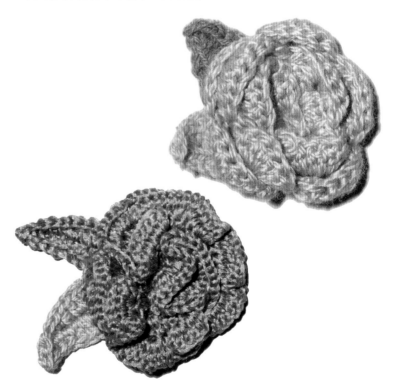

# Cloche Hat

Skill Level:
Basic

A casual
day look is
enlivened by
a burst of
colour in this
lime crochet
cloche hat,
inspired by
a version by
Marc Jacobs,
opposite. The
1920s feel of
the hat is
enhanced by
the geometric
Art Deco-style
button.

## Cloche Hat
Claire Montgomerie

A cloche is a classic
piece that has
yet again hit the
catwalks, proving its
timeless appeal and
easy elegance for
everyday wear. Make
it in a tweed yarn, as
pictured, for a casual
day look, or use a
block colour to make
a striking statement
piece for day or night.

## YARN

2 x 50g (2 oz) balls of Rowan Felted Tweed DK, 50% merino wool, 25% alpaca, 25% viscose, 175 m (191 yds) in shade 161, avocado

## NOTIONS

4 mm (size 8) crochet hook
3.5 mm (size 9) crochet hook
Button (for decoration only, optional)
Tapestry needle

## MEASUREMENTS

One size, to fit average female adult head, approx 52–56 cm (20–22 in) in circumference.

## TENSION/GAUGE

18htr and 14 rows to 10 cm (4 in) using a 4 mm (size 8) hook or size required to obtain correct tension.

## PATTERN

The hat is worked in the round, joining each rnd with a sl st to the top of first ch of rnd. All starting chains of each round count as first htr or dc.

**Rnd 1:** Using 4mm (size 8) hook, work 8htr into a magic loop and join for working in the round.
**Rnd 2:** ch2, 2htr into each st around, join rnd to top of first ch. *16 htr.*
**Rnd 3:** ch2, 2htr into first st, (1htr, 2htr into next st) to end of rnd, join rnd. *24 htr.*
**Rnd 4:** ch2, 2htr into first st, (2htr, 2htr into next st) to end of rnd, join rnd. *32 htr.*
**Rnd 5:** ch2, 2htr into first st, (3htr, 2htr into next st) to end of rnd, join rnd. *40 htr.*
**Rnd 6:** ch2, 2htr into first st, (4htr, 2htr into next st) to end of rnd, join rnd. *48 htr.*
**Rnd 7:** ch2, 2htr into first st, (5htr, 2htr into next st) to end of rnd, join rnd. *56 htr.*
**Rnd 8:** ch2, 2htr into first st, (6htr, 2htr into next st) to end of rnd, join rnd. *64 htr.*
**Rnd 9:** Work one rnd straight without increasing.
**Rnd 10:** ch2, 2htr into first st, (7htr, 2htr into next st) to end of rnd, join rnd. *72 htr.*

Continue increasing in the same way, with one rnd straight in between each increase row until there are 96htr.

Work straight for 11 rows or until desired depth to brim.

### Brim
Change to 3.5mm (size 9) hook and work one row straight in htr.
Work 3 rows straight in dc.
Work one further row in htr.
Change back to 4 mm (size 8) hook.

**Next row:** ch2, 2htr into first st, (7htr, 2htr into next st) to end of rnd, join rnd. *108 htr.*
**Next row:** ch2, 2htr into first st, (8htr, 2htr into next st) to end of rnd, join rnd. *120 htr.*

**Next row:** ch2, 2htr into first st, (9htr, 2htr into next st) to end of rnd, join rnd. *132 htr.*
Fasten off yarn.

Using yarn held double and 4 mm (size 8) hook, work 8ch.

Work 1tr into 3rd ch from hook, then 1tr into each ch to end. *5tr.*

**Row 1:** 3ch, (rtrf, rtrb) twice. Turn.
**Row 2:** 3ch, (rtrb, rtrf) twice. Turn.
Rep these two rows until strip measures circumference of hat just above rim, with a slight overlap.
Fasten off yarn.

### Finishing
Attach strip to hat just above the brim, overlapping at one end slightly and stitching on a button for detail.

Substitute one – or several – of the flower corsages on pages 68–73 for the button if you want a more feminine style.

# Bobble Bag

**Skill Level:**
**Intermediate**

The Gerard
Darel
"Syracuse"
24-Hour Bag,
as worn by
Angelina
Jolie,
opposite,
features a
lovely diamond
bobble pattern
that is re-
interpreted in
the design of
this small,
pouch-shaped
handbag,
right.

## Bobble Bag
Zoë Clements

This lovely little bag
is made in a soft,
subtly glittery, alpaca-
blend yarn called
Flicker that lends just
a hint of shimmer to
the bag, making it
perfect for an evening
out. The bobbles
are easy to work
but look stunning
and complicated
when used to create
a geometric relief
pattern.

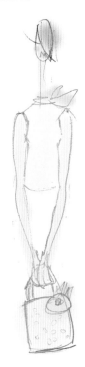

## YARN

3 x 50 g (2 oz) balls of Berrocco Flicker, 87%
   baby alpaca, 8% acrylic, 5% other fibres,
   173 m (189 yds) in shade 3320, cygne

## NOTIONS

4 mm (size 8) crochet hook
Tapestry needle

## MEASUREMENTS

One size, measuring 28 x 23 cm (11 x 9 in)

## TENSION/GAUGE

Work 18 sts and 17 rows in Diamond Bobble pattern
to measure 10 x 10 cm (4 x 4in). Exact tension is not
essential for this project, but should remain consistent
to retain shape.

## SPECIAL INSTRUCTIONS

**Bobble Stitch:** yrh, insert hook in required stitch,
*yrh, pull up a loop, yrh, pull through 2 loops, yrh,
insert hook in same st; rep from * 4 times, yrh, pull
up a loop, pull through 2 loops, yrh, pull through all
remaining loops on hook.

## PATTERN
### Body of the Bag
Make 2.
Using a 4 mm (size 8) hook, ch43.

**Row 1:** Work 1tr in 4th ch from hook, 1tr in each ch
to end. Turn. *41 sts.*
**Row 2 (and all even rows):** 1ch (does not count as a st
now and throughout), 1dc in each st across. *41 sts.*
**Row 3:** 3ch (counts as 1 tr now and throughout), 7tr,
bobble, 11tr, bobble, 11tr, bobble, 8tr. Turn.
**Row 5:** ch3, 5tr, bobble, 3tr, bobble, 7tr, *bobble,
1tr; rep from * 1 more time, bobble, 7tr, bobble, 3tr,
bobble, 6tr. Turn.
**Row 7:** ch3, 3tr, bobble, 7tr, bobble, 3tr, *bobble,
1tr; rep from * 3 more times, bobble, 3tr, bobble, 7tr,
bobble, 4tr. Turn.
**Row 9:** ch3, 1tr, bobble, 11tr, *bobble, 1tr; rep from
* 5 more times, bobble, 11tr, bobble, 2tr. Turn.

KEY

⬡ 5 treble crochet cluster     ◠ chain stitch     + double crochet     ┳ treble crochet     ⋀ tr2tog - treble crochet 2 together

**Row 11:** Rep row 7.
**Row 13:** Rep row 5.
**Row 15:** Rep row 3.
**Row 17:** ch3, 5tr, *bobble, 1tr; rep from * 1 more time, bobble**, 7tr, bobble, 3tr, bobble, 7tr, rep from * to **, 6tr. Turn.
**Row 19:** ch3, 3tr, *bobble, 1tr; rep from * 3 more times, bobble**, 3tr, bobble, 7tr, bobble, 3tr, rep from * to **, 4tr. Turn.
**Row 21:** ch3, 1tr, *bobble, 1tr; rep from * 5 more times, bobble**, 11tr, rep from * to **, 2tr. Turn.
**Row 23:** Rep row 19.
**Row 25:** Rep row 17.
**Row 27:** Rep row 15.
**Rows 29–33:** Rep rows 5–9.

Decreases begin.
**Row 35:** ch2, 1tr (counts as tr2tog decrease now and throughout), tr2tog, bobble, 7tr, bobble, 3tr, *bobble, 1tr; rep from * 3 more times, bobble, 3tr, bobble, 7tr, bobble, tr2tog twice. Turn.
**Row 37:** ch2, 1tr, tr2tog, bobble, 3tr, bobble, 7tr, *bobble, 1tr; rep from * 1 more time, bobble, 7tr, bobble, 3tr, bobble, tr2tog twice. Turn.
**Row 39:** ch2, 1tr, tr2tog, bobble, 11tr, bobble, 11tr, bobble, tr2tog twice.
**Row 40:** ch1, dc across.
Fasten off.

**Straps**
Rejoin yarn to first st at the right-hand top of bag piece, after the decreases, on the RS.

Work straps as follows:
**Row 1:** ch3, 1tr in next st, bobble, 2tr. Turn.
**Row 2:** ch3, tr across. Turn.
Repeat last two rows until strap reaches desired length. Fasten off.

Firmly sew the loose end of the strap to the last 5 sts on the left-hand side (before decreases) of the body piece.

Repeat for the other body piece.

**Finishing**
Weave in ends.
Block gently.
Seam sides together, making sure that the bobbles match.

# Straw-Inspired Tote

Skill Level:
Basic

This flower-adorned tote, inspired by traditional straw market bags and the Chanel crochet bag seen in the Spring/ Summer 2010 ensemble, opposite, makes a lovely accessory to summery outfits.

## Straw-Inspired Tote

Zoë Clements

Traditional straw bags are often crocheted and this bag has a nod to those practical shoppers – it would look fabulous on the beach or at the grocery store. If you wish, add even more flowers for a cheery look.

## YARN

3 x 100 g (4 oz) balls of Blue Sky Alpacas worsted
   cotton, 100% organic cotton, 137 m (150 yd) in
   shade 608, lemonade

1 x 100 g (4 oz) ball each of Blue Sky Alpacas
   worsted cotton, 100% organic cotton, 137 m
   (150 yd) in shade 637, raspberry (yarn A);
   shade 632, Mediterranean (yarn B); shade 634,
   periwinkle (yarn C); shade 617, lotus (yarn D)

## NOTIONS

4 mm (size 8) crochet hook
3.5 mm (size 9) crochet hook
Lockable stitch marker
Tapestry needle
127 cm (50 in) x 6 mm (¼ in) co-ordinating ribbon
82 cm (32 in) waste yarn

## MEASUREMENT

One size, approximately 28 x 37 cm (11 x 14½ in)

## TENSION

Work 21 rows and 16 sts in dc to measure 10 x 10
cm (4 x 4 in).

## SPECIAL INSTRUCTIONS

**Raised dc back (RdcB)** = Work a dc as follows:
Keeping the hook at the back of the work, insert the
hook from right to left around the "legs" of the dc in the
row below. Yrh, pull up a loop, yrh, pull through both
loops on hook.

TIP: Use the lockable stitch marker to help keep track
of the ends of rounds, remembering to move it up
each round as you go.

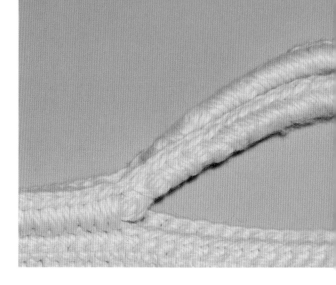

## PATTERN
### Body of the Bag
Using 4 mm (size 8) hook and in shade 608, ch31.

Switch to 3.5 mm (size 9) hook and work as follows:
**Rnd 1:** Work 1dc in 2nd ch from hook, dc in each ch across to last ch, 4dc in last ch. Working along the underside of the ch, 1dc in each ch across to last ch, 3dc in last ch, join to first dc with a sl st.
**Rnd 2:** 1ch (does not count as a st now and throughout), *30dc, 2dc in each of next 3 sts; rep from *, join to first dc with a sl st.
**Rnd 3:** 1ch, *32dc, 2dc in next st, (2dc, 2dc in next st) twice; rep from *, join to first dc with a sl st.
**Rnd 4:** 1ch, *31dc, 2dc in next st, 2dc, (1dc, 2dc in next st, 2dc) twice; rep from *, join to first dc with a sl st.
**Rnd 5:** 1ch, *34dc, 2dc in next st, (4dc, 2dc in next st) twice; rep from *, join to first dc with a sl st.
**Rnd 6:** 1ch, *33dc, 2dc in next st, 2dc, (3dc, 2dc in next st, 2dc) twice; rep from *, join to first dc with a sl st.
**Rnd 7:** 1ch, dc in each st around, sl st to first dc to join.

From this point on, turn the work at the end of each round (after the sl st join).

**Rnd 8:** ch1, RdcB across, sl st to first dc to join. Turn.
**Rnd 9–13:** ch1, dc across, sl st to first dc to join. Turn.
**Rnd 14:** ch1, dc39, 2dc in next st, 1dc, 2dc in next st, dc39, sl st to first dc to join. Turn.
**Rnds 15–20:** Rep rnd 9.
**Rnd 21:** dc40, 2dc in next st, 1dc, 2dc in next st, 40dc, sl st to first dc to join. Turn.
**Rnds 22–28:** Rep rnd 9.
**Rnd 29:** ch1, dc41, 2dc in next st, 1dc, 2dc in next st, dc41, sl st to first dc to join. Turn.
**Rnds 30–37:** Rep rnd 9.
**Rnd 38:** ch1, dc42, 2dc in next st, 1dc, 2dc in next st, dc42, sl st to first dc to join. Turn.
**Rnds 39–47:** Rep rnd 9.
**Rnd 48:** ch1, dc43, 2dc in next st, 1dc, 2dc in next st, dc43, sl st to first dc to join. Turn.

**Rnds 49–54:** Rep rnd 9.
**Rnd 55:** ch4 (counts as 1tr, 1ch), miss next st, *1tr in next st, 1ch, miss next st; rep from * around, sl st to 3rd ch of t-ch. Turn.
**Rnd 56:** ch1, dc in each tr and ch-sp around, sl st to first dc. Turn.
**Rnds 57–60:** Rep rnd 9.

### Handle
Cut an 82 cm (32 in) length of waste yarn and tie in a circle. Using this as a template, take the other end of the ball, and wrap the yarn around in a circle until it is approximately 1.3 cm (½ in) thick. Cut, and tie in places to secure.

Holding the circle and the bag body, work dcs around the circle and into the sts from rnd 60. Leave a gap for your hand in the side, by working dcs around the circle only, then continue working into the rnd 60 sts when required. Make sure that the dcs are tightly packed in the hand gap section, as this will give additional strength.

Continue working dcs around, leaving a matching hand gap on the other side, and sl st to first dc when round is complete.

Fasten off.

### Flowers

Make 4.

Using yarns A–D (or scrap yarn if preferred) work as follows:

Make an adjustable loop and sl st to secure.

**ch 3, *yrh, insert hook into ring, pull up a loop, yrh, pull through 2 loops; rep from * 2 more times, yrh, pull through all loops on hook, ch3, sl st into ring; rep from ** 7 more times. Fasten off.

### Finishing

Weave in ends and block gently.

Attach flowers in desired places, using tapestry needle and matching yarn.

Thread ribbon through tr section and tie in a bow.

# Chain
Shoulder Bag

**Skill Level:
Basic**

These pretty
contrasting
flowers can
be reproduced
and used all
over the bag,
as with the
beautiful
Stella
MaCartney
Falabella
bag, opposite,
which
inspired this
version, or
even omitted
entirely
for a chic
and simple
everyday
shopper.

## Chain Shoulder Bag
Zoë Clements

Incorporating non-traditional materials within crocheted accessories is very contemporary and will make any bag truly unique. The chains worked into the shoulder strap of this stunning bag strengthen the strap and make an interesting feature.

## YARN

3 x 100 g (4 oz) balls of Rowan Creative linen,
50% linen, 50% cotton, 200 m (219 yds) in
shade 622, straw
1 x 100 g (4 oz) ball of Rowan Creative linen,
50% linen, 50% cotton, 200 m (219 yds) in
shade 621, natural

## NOTIONS

4 mm (size 8) crochet hook
5 mm (size 6) crochet hook
Tapestry needle
1.25 m (1.36 yd) chain, available from
hardware stores)
Pliers (for joining the chain)

## MEASUREMENTS

One size, measuring approximately 46 x 42 cm
(18 x 16½ in)

## TENSION/GAUGE

Tension is not crucial for this project, but should remain
consistent to retain shape.

## PATTERN NOTES

Please note that while the pattern is worked in rounds,
some of the rounds need to be turned and worked
in the other direction. This is indicated in the pattern.
Please do not turn the work unless instructed to do so.

## PATTERN

### Body of the Bag

Using 4 mm (size 8) hook and shade 622, ch61.

**Rnd 1:** Work 1tr in 4th ch from hook, 1tr in each ch to last ch, 2tr in last ch, turning to work on the underside of the ch, work 1tr in each ch to last ch, 2tr in last ch, sl st to 3rd ch of t-ch to join. *120 sts.*
**Rnd 2:** 3ch (counts as 1tr now and throughout), 54tr, 3tr in next st, 55tr, 3tr in next st, sl st to t-ch to join. *124 sts.*
**Rnd 3:** 3ch, 54tr, 2tr in next st, 1tr, 2tr in next st, 55tr, 2tr in next st, 1tr, 2tr in next st, sl st to 3rd ch of t-ch to join. *128 sts.*
**Rnd 4:** ch3, 1tr in each st across to end, join to 3rd ch of t-ch with a sl st. Turn.
**Rnds 4–24:** Rep rnd 3.
Fasten off.

### Handle

Counting from the stitch fastened off, miss 32tr, rejoin yarn to 33rd tr and work as follows:
**\*\*Row 1:** ch2, 1tr (counts as tr2tog decrease now and throughout), tr2tog, 56tr, tr2tog twice\*. Turn.
**Row 2:** ch2, 1tr, tr2tog, 52tr, tr2tog twice. Turn.
**Row 3:** ch2, 1tr, tr2tog, 48tr, tr2tog twice. Turn.

Continue decreasing in this way, reducing the number of trebles worked each row by 4, until 4 trebles remain between decreases.

**Next Row:** ch3, tr across. Turn.

Repeat last row 14 more times. Fasten off.\*\*

Rejoin yarn to bag body, in the st next to the last st worked in Row 1 (indicated with a \*) above. Repeat from \*\* to \*\*.

### Chain Strap

Fold the last row of trs on each strap back over the previous row, and stitch (or crochet) in place. This provides additional strength and support for the strap. This step may be omitted if the bag is being lined with fabric.

Thread the chain through the spaces between the trs on each side, in a zig-zag fashion.

When you are happy with the chain strap, use the pliers to open a link on either side, join, and close the link.

### Large Flower

Using shade 621, and 5 mm (size 6) hook, make an adjustable loop. Sl st to secure.

**Rnd 1:** ch4, \*1tr in ring, 1ch; rep from \* 6 more times, sl st to 3rd ch of t-ch.
**Rnd 2:** ch3 (counts as 1tr now and throughout), 1tr in base of ch, \*3ch, 2tr in next tr; rep from \*6 more times, 2ch, sl st to 3rd ch of t-ch to join.

The chain, above, adds strength to the handle, which is necessary for this voluminous, oversized bag. The neutral colours make the bag a versatile choice for the wardrobe, but for a different look, stitch the flowers in a contrasting rather than tonal shade to that of the bag.

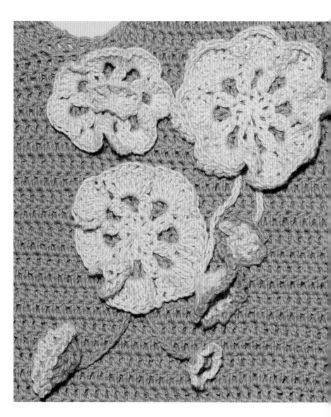

**Rnd 3:** sl st across to next 3ch-sp, ch3, tr in ch-sp, 1ch, *7tr in next ch-sp, 1ch; rep from * 5 more times, sl st to 3rd ch of t-ch to join.

**Rnd 4:** 1ch, dc in top of t-ch, *2htr in next st, 2tr in next st, 2dtr in next st, 2tr in next st, 2htr in next st, 1dc in next st, miss 1ch-sp**, 1dc in next st; rep from around, ending last repeat at **, sl st to first dc to join.

Fasten off. Pull tail on adjustable loop to tighten.

## Medium Flower
Work rnds 1–3 of Large Flower, using 4 mm (size 8) hook and shade 621.

## Small Flower
Work rnd 1 of Large Flower, using 4 mm (size 8) hook and shade 621.

## Large Flower Stamen
Using shade 621, and 4 mm (size 8) hook, make a length of chain for the filament – varying the lengths work well for the overall design. sl st to 6th ch from hook (forming the anther).

**Rnd 1:** ch3, work 5tr into same ch as sl st, sl st to 3rd ch of t-ch to join.

**Rnd 2:** ch3, 1tr in base of ch, 2tr in each tr around, sl st to 3rd ch of t-ch to secure.
Fasten off.
Attach shade 622 to any tr, 1ch, dc in each tr around, sl st to first dc to secure.
Fasten off.

## Small Flower Stamen
Repeat as for the Large Flower Stamen but omit rnd 2.

## Finishing
Weave in ends.
Block gently.
Attach stamens in desired places, using a tapestry needle and the corresponding colour of yarn.

Little Black Dress

Poolside Dress

Tunic Dress

# dresses, skirts & shorts

Summer Mini Skirt

Monochrome
Granny-Square Skirt

Beach Shorts

## Little Black Dress

Skill Level:
Advanced

Everyone needs
a little black
dress and
this one is
versatile - it
can be worn
with bright
tights and
sky-high heels
for a unique,
on-trend
evening outfit
or paired with
comfortable
court shoes
for work. Like
the crocheted
Dolce &
Gabbana dress,
opposite,
this version
is a great
alternative
to a black
lace dress.

## Little Black Dress
Claire Montgomerie

A classic little black
dress will never go
out of fashion. The
yoke and sleeves
are worked with an
open pretty floral
stitch as a contrast
to the elegance of
the dense, figure-
hugging, main body,
while mismatched
sparkly glass and
pearl buttons are
added to the back
opening for a touch of
glamour. These could
be substituted with
matching buttons for
a more sedate look.

## YARN
16 [18:19:20] x 50 g (2 oz) balls of Bessie May
Smitsy, 100% fine merino washable wool, 75 m
(82 yds) in shade 2160, nero

## NOTIONS
5 mm (size 6) crochet hook
12 assorted buttons
Stitch markers
Tapestry needle

## MEASUREMENTS (to fit with negative ease)
Bust

| | | | |
|---|---|---|---|
| 81 | 86 | 91 | 96 cm |
| 32 | 34 | 36 | 38 in |

Waist

| | | | |
|---|---|---|---|
| 64 | 67 | 71 | 76 cm |
| 25 | 26½ | 28 | 30 in |

Length
95 cm
37½ in

## TENSION/GAUGE
17 sts and 17 rows in main pattern to 10 x 10 cm
(4 x 4 in) using 5 mm (size 6) hook or size to obtain
correct tension.

## PATTERN NOTES
Where the skirt of dress is worked in the round, do not
join end of rounds, but work in spirals, placing a stitch
marker to mark start of round

## SPECIAL INSTRUCTIONS

**Petal Stitch:** yrh twice, insert hook into st, pull through lp, yrh, pull through 2 lps, yrh pull through 2 lps, 2 lps rem on hook, yrh twice, insert hook into same st, pull through lp, yrh, pull through 2 lps, yrh pull through 2 lps, 3 lps rem on hook, yrh twice, insert hook into same st, pull through lp, yrh, pull through 2 lps, yrh pull through 2 lps, 4 lps rem on hook, pull through all rem loops. Petal made.

**2 Unfinished dtr:** yrh twice, insert hook into st, pull through lp, yrh, pull through 2 lps, yrh pull through 2 lps, 2 lps rem on hook, yrh twice, insert hook into same st, pull through lp, yrh, pull through 2 lps, yrh pull through 2 lps, 3 lps rem on hook, pull through all rem loops.

KEY

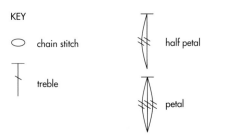

⬭ chain stitch

┬ treble

half petal

petal

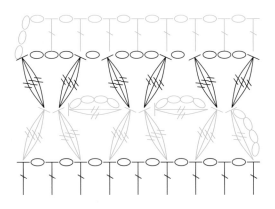

## PATTERN

Using 5 mm (size 6) hook, ch 144[140:152:160] and join with a sl st to first ch for working in the rnd.

**Rnd 1:** ch2 (to count as dc, ch1), *miss next ch, (dc, 1ch) into next ch; rep from * to end of rnd. Do not join round.

**Rnd 2:** miss first dc, *(dc, 1ch) into next 1 ch sp, miss next dc; rep from * to end of rnd. Do not join round.

**Rnd 3:** *(dc, 1ch) into next ch sp, miss next dc; rep from * to end of rnd. Do not join round.

Last two rnds form pattern for dress skirt, repeat these, working in spirals until skirt measures 40 cm (15¾ in) from hem, ending with a rnd 3.

### Begin decreasing for waist as follows:

**Dec rnd:** (1ch, dc into ch sp) 8 times, *1ch, miss (next dc, ch sp, dc), dc into next ch sp, 2 sts decreased, (1ch, dc) 16 times; rep from * twice more, 1ch, miss (next dc, ch sp, dc), dc into next ch sp, 2 sts decreased, pattern to end of rnd. *136[132:144:152] sts.*
Work 9 rnds straight in pattern on these sts.

**Dec rnd:** dc, (1ch, dc into ch sp) 7 times, *1ch, miss (next dc, ch sp, dc), dc into next ch sp, two sts decreased, (1ch, dc into ch sp) 15 times; rep from * twice more, 1ch, miss (next dc, ch sp, dc), dc into next ch sp, two sts decreased, pattern to end of rnd. *128[132:136:144] sts.*
Work 9 rnds straight in pattern on these sts.

**Dec rnd:** (1ch, dc into ch sp) 7 times, *1ch, miss (next dc, ch sp, dc), dc into next ch sp, two sts decreased, (1ch, dc into ch sp) 14 times; rep from * twice more, 1ch, miss (next dc, ch sp, dc), dc into next ch sp, two sts decreased, pattern to end of rnd. *120[124:128:136] sts.*
Work 9 rnds straight in pattern on these sts.

**Dec rnd:** dc, (1ch, dc into ch sp) 6 times, *1ch, miss (next dc, ch sp, dc), dc into next ch sp, two sts decreased, (1ch, dc into ch sp) 13 times; rep from *

twice more, 1ch, miss (next dc, ch sp, dc), dc into next ch sp, two sts decreased, pattern to end of rnd, working an extra dc into last st. *113[117:121:129] sts.*
Turn.

### Working straight from now on for back opening.
Work 7 rows straight without decreasing, turning every rnd as folls:

**Row 1:** 1ch, dc into first ch sp, (1ch, dc into next ch sp) to end, finishing with a dc into last dc. Turn.

**Row 2:** 2ch (counts as dc and ch) dc into first ch sp, (1ch, dc into ch sp) to end, finishing 1ch, dc into last dc.
Rep last 2 rows for pattern from now on, rep last 2 rows twice more, then row 1 again.

**Inc rnd:** 1ch (1ch, dc into ch sp) 6 times, (1ch, dc 1ch) into next dc (inc made), *dc into next ch sp, (1ch, dc into ch sp) 13 times, (1ch, dc 1ch) into next dc; rep from * twice more, pattern to end of row. *121[125:129:137] sts.*
Work 8 rows in pattern without increasing.

**Inc rnd:** 1ch, dc into first ch sp, (1ch, dc into next ch sp) 6 times, (1ch, dc 1ch) into next dc (inc made), * dc into next ch sp, (1ch, dc into ch sp) 14 times, (1ch, dc 1ch) into next dc; rep from * twice more, pattern to end of row. *128[133:137:145] sts.*
Work 8 rows in pattern without increasing.

**Inc rnd:** 1ch (1ch, dc into ch sp) 7 times, (1ch, dc 1ch) into next dc (inc made), *dc into next ch sp, (1ch, dc into ch sp) 15 times, (1ch, dc 1ch) into next dc; rep from * twice more, pattern to end of row. *136[141:145:153] sts.*
Work 8 rows in pattern without increasing.

**Inc rnd:** 1ch, dc into first ch sp, (1ch, dc into next ch sp) 7 times, (1ch, dc 1ch) into next dc (inc made), * dc into next ch sp, (1ch, dc into ch sp) 16 times, (1ch, dc 1ch) into next dc; rep from * twice more, pattern to end of row. *144[149:153:161] sts.*
Work straight in pattern without shaping until piece measures 26[26:27:27] cm (10¼ [10¼:10⅔:10⅔] in) from back opening, ending with a WSR.

### Back Armhole Shaping

**Next row:** Work across 30[31:31:33]sts, turn, leaving rem sts unworked.

**Next row:** dec 1 st at beg of row, work to end of row. Work 2 further rows, decreasing 1 st at armhole edge of each row.

Work straight until left back measures 17[17.5:18:18.5] cm (6 ⅔ [6 ⅔: 7: 7 ¼] in) from beginning of armhole shaping, ending with WSR.

### Shoulder Shaping

**Next row:** Work across 23[24:24:26]sts, leaving rem 4[4:4:5]sts unworked.

**Next row:** sl st across 3[3:3:4]sts, work to end.

**Next row:** Work across 3 sts, leaving rem sts unworked.

Fasten off yarn.

Reattach yarn to right back armhole and work to match left back, reversing all shapings.

### Armhole Shaping

Reattach yarn to left front armhole with RSF, 12[12:14:14]sts along from left back armhole, work across 60[63:63:67]sts, turn, leaving rem sts unworked for armhole.

Work straight in pattern for 3 rows, decreasing 1[2:2:1]sts at both ends of first row and 1 st at both ends of every foll row. *54[55:55:61]sts.*

### Yoke

**Row 1:** 4ch (counts as 1tr, 1ch), miss next 2[1:1:1]sts, 1tr into next st, *1ch, miss next st, 1tr into next st; rep from * to end of row. Turn.

**Row 2:** 4ch (counts as 1tr, 1ch), 1tr into next tr, *1ch, 1tr into next tr; rep from * to end of row. Turn.

**Row 3:** ch 4 (counts as 1dtr) 2 unfinished dtr into bottom of ch, miss next tr, petal into next tr, *4ch, 2 unfinished dtr into bottom of ch, petal into next tr, miss next tr, petal into next tr; rep from * to end of row. Turn.

**Row 4:** ch 4 (counts as 1dtr) 2 unfinished dtr into bottom of ch, 3ch, petal into petal, *1ch, (petal, 3ch, petal) into next petal; rep from * to end of row. Turn.

**Row 5:** 4ch (counts as 1tr, 1ch), 1tr into 2nd of 3ch, 1ch, 1tr into next petal 1ch, 1tr into next petal, 1ch, tr into 2nd of 3ch, 1ch, 1tr into next petal, turn leaving rem sts unworked.

**Row 6:** 4ch (counts as 1tr, 1ch), 1tr into next tr, *1ch, 1tr into next tr; rep from * to end of row. Turn.

Rep last row until work measures same as back to shoulder shaping.

Working in dc, work shoulder shaping to match back. Reattach yarn to opposite side of yoke and work to match left side, reversing all shaping.

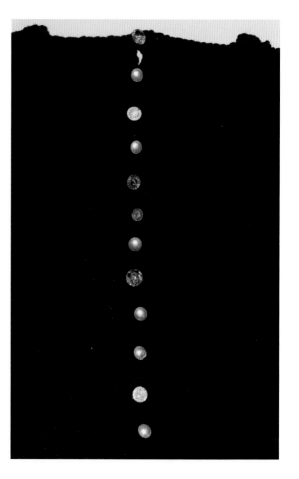

## Sleeves

Using 5 mm (size 6) hook, ch45[45:51:51].

**Row 1:** Work 1tr into 4th ch from hook, then work1tr into each ch to end of row. Turn. *41[41:47:47]tr.*

**Row 2:** 4ch (counts as 1tr, 1ch), miss next st, 1tr into next st, *1ch, miss next st, 1tr into next st; rep from * to end of row. Turn.

**Row 3:** 4ch (counts as 1tr, 1ch), 1tr into next tr, *1ch, 1tr into next tr; rep from * to end of row. Turn.

**Row 4:** as last row.

**Row 5:** ch 4 (counts as 1dtr) 2 unfinished dtr into bottom of ch, miss next tr, petal into next tr, *4ch, 2 unfinished dtr into bottom of ch, petal into next tr, miss next tr, petal into next tr; rep from * to end of row. Turn.

**Row 6:** ch 4 (counts as 1dtr) 2 unfinished dtr into bottom of ch, petal into petal, *1ch, (petal, 3ch, petal) into next petal; rep from * to end of row. Turn.

**Row 7:** 4ch (counts as 1tr, 1ch), *1tr into 2nd of 3ch, 1ch, 1tr into next petal 1ch, 1tr into next petal; rep from * to end of row.

**Row 8:** as row 3.

**Rows 9 and 10:** Rep rows 5 and 6.

**Row 11:** as row 7.

**Row 12:** sl st across 3 filet spaces, work in filet to last 3 spaces, turn, leaving these 3 spaces unworked.

Work a further 3 rows in fliet, decreasing 1 space at both ends of each row.

Work a further 3 rows straight in filet.

Fasten off yarn.

## Finishing

Block all pieces lightly to shape.

Sew up shoulder seams and set in sleeves.

Sew buttons at even intervals down left back edge.

Attach yarn to right back opening at neck. Work 1dc down edge, *work a chain the correct length to fasten top button, miss 1 row down the edge, then work 1dc into next row, work dc evenly down edge to next button position; rep from * to bottom of edge.

Fasten off yarn.

Weave in all ends.

Block all seams lightly to set.

# Tunic Dress

Skill Level:
Intermediate

The colours
and openwork
styling of
this off-the-
shoulder tunic
was inspired
by the cut-
out bubble-
hem strapless
dress by
Ashley Isham,
far right,
and a chevron
Missoni dress,
opposite.

## Tunic Dress
Claire Montgomerie

The 1960s is a
decade that is a
constant source
of inspiration for
modern designers
and shift and tunic-
style dresses and tops
inspired by this era
feature heavily on
the catwalk, creating
looks suitable for any
season. This dress is
perfect for summer but
can easily be layered
over trousers for the
cooler months.

## YARN

9[11:12:14] balls of MillaMia Naturally Soft Merino, 100% merino, 125 m (137 yds) in shade 104, claret (yarn A)

1 x 50 g (2 oz) ball of MillaMia Naturally Soft Merino, 100% merino, 125 m (137 yds) in shade 140, scarlet (yarn B)

## NOTIONS

3.5[3.75:4:4.5] mm (size 9[9:8:7]) crochet hook
Tapestry needle

## MEASUREMENTS

Bust

| 32 | 34 | 36 | 38 in |
| 81 | 86 | 91 | 96 cm |

Actual Size

| 35¾ | 37¾ | 39¾ | 41¾ in |
| 88 | 96 | 100 | 104 cm |

Length

| 68 | 72 | 76 | 80 cm |
| 27 | 28¼ | 30 | 31½ in |

## TENSION/GAUGE

Each motif is approx 11[12:12.5:13] cm (4¼[4¾:5:5¼] in) in diameter using 3.5 mm (size 9) hook or size required to obtain correct tension.

## PATTERN NOTES

The measurements allow for stretching.
Extra rounds of motifs can be added as desired to lengthen the tunic.

## SPECIAL INSTRUCTIONS

**Extended Chain (e-ch):** 1ch and extend ch to height of htr; does not count as stitch.

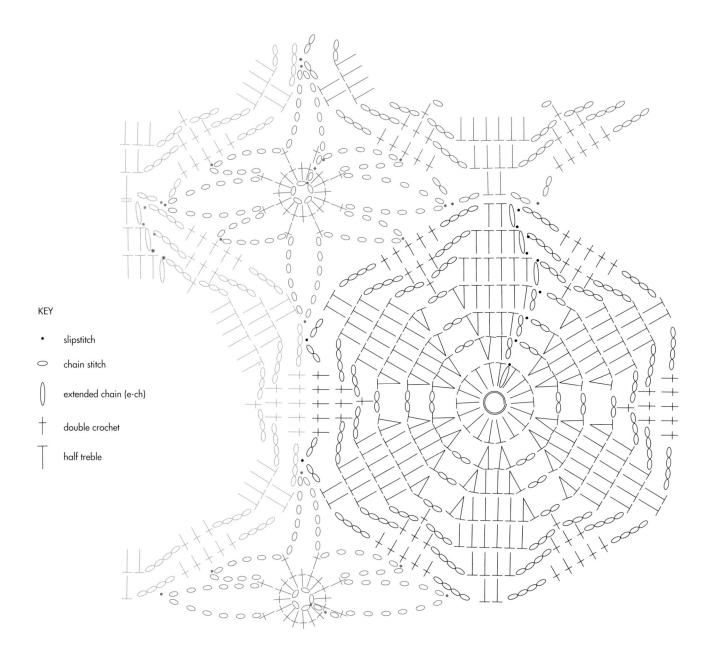

KEY

•    slipstitch

◯    chain stitch

◊    extended chain (e-ch)

†    double crochet

⊤    half treble

## PATTERN
### First Motif
Using 3.5(3.75:4:4.5) mm hook and yarn B, make magic ring, e-ch, work 18htr into a magic ring, pull up tight to fasten and join rnd with a sl st.
Change to yarn A.

**Rnd 2:** 2ch, htr into bottom of ch, 2htr into next st, 2ch, miss next htr, *(2htr into next st) twice, 2ch, miss next htr, rep from * around, join rnd with a sl st.
**Rnd 3:** ch 2, htr into bottom of chain, 2htr, 2htr into next htr, 2ch, *2htr into next htr, 2htr, 2htr into next htr, 2ch; rep from * to end of rnd, join with a sl st.
**Rnd 4:** 2ch, htr into bottom of chain, 4htr, 2htr into next htr, 2ch, *2htr into next htr, 4htr, 2htr into next htr, 2ch; rep from * to end of rnd, join with a sl st.
**Rnd 5:** e-ch, miss htr, 6htr, miss next htr, 3ch, 1dc into 2ch sp, 3ch, *miss next htr, 6htr, miss next htr, 3ch, 1dc into 2ch sp, 3ch; rep from * to end of rnd, sl st to join rnd.
**Rnd 6:** e-ch, miss htr, 4htr, miss next htr, 4ch, 1dc into 3ch sp, 1dc, 1dc into 3ch sp, 4ch, *miss next htr, 4htr, miss next htr, 4ch, 1dc into 3ch sp, 1dc, 1dc into 3ch sp, 4ch; rep from * to end of rnd, sl st to join rnd.
**Rnd 7:** e-ch, miss htr, 2htr, miss next htr, 4ch, 1dc into 4ch sp, 3dc, 1dc into 4ch sp, 4ch, *miss next htr, 2htr, miss next htr, 4ch, 1dc into 4ch sp, 3dc, 1dc into 4ch sp, 4ch; rep from * to end of rnd, sl st to join rnd. Fasten off yarn.

Make next motif in same way to rnd 6.

Place unfinished motif 2 to right of motif one, with RS facing (see chart opposite).

**Rnd 7:** sl st in next htr, 2htr, miss next htr, 2ch, sl st to centre of corresponding 4ch of motif one, 2ch, 1dc into 4ch sp, 3dc, 1dc into 4ch sp, 2ch, sl st to centre of corresponding 4ch of motif one, 2ch, *miss next htr, 2htr, miss next htr, 4ch, 1dc into 4ch sp, 3dc, 1dc into 4ch sp, 4ch; rep from * to end of rnd, sl st to join rnd. Fasten off yarn.

Make 6 further motifs, joining in the same way, joining

8th motif to both 7th and first motif on the final round to create complete hem of dress. This completes the 8 motifs for the hem round of the dress.

All rem motifs will be worked completely in yarn A. there will be a total of 40 motifs solely in yarn A, which is a total of 48 motifs for the entire dress.

Each new motif worked will be joined as you go to the motif next to it on the 7th round, as in the hem, but also joined to the motif below it, working the dress round by round up from the hem.

Work each of the yarn A motifs exactly as the hem motifs, but just in yarn A, up to rnd 6.

Join to motif beside and below it as follows (see chart):
**Rnd 7:** sl st across next htr, 2htr, miss next htr, 2ch, sl st to centre of corresponding 4ch of previous motif, 2ch, 1dc into 4ch sp, 3dc, 1dc into 4ch sp, 2ch, sl st to centre of corresponding 4ch of previous motif, 2ch, miss next htr, 2htr, miss next htr, 4ch, 1dc into 4ch sp, 3dc, 1dc into 4ch sp, 2ch, sl st to centre of corresponding 4ch of motif directly below this, 2ch, miss next htr, 2htr, miss next htr, 2ch, sl st to centre of corresponding 4ch of motif directly below this, 2ch, 1dc into 4ch sp, 3dc, 1dc into 4ch sp, 4ch, *miss next htr, 2htr, miss next htr, 4ch, 1dc into 4ch sp, 3dc, 1dc into 4ch sp, 4ch; rep from * to end of rnd, sl st to join rnd. Fasten off yarn.

The first motifs that form the hem of the skirt are worked in scarlet magic rings while all the other motifs are worked solidly in claret yarn. For a more extroverted effect, make all the motifs with scarlet centres.

With last motif of round, join to motif on either side as well as below, to join into round.

When you reach the final round (round 6, shoulders and neck), join central two motifs of front and back as normal, but to make armhole, join motifs skewed as follows:
Join first motif of round to motif below, and next two motifs of round to motif to the left and motif below as normal. 4th motif of rnd make the armhole on rnd 7 joining rnd, ensure that where you start rnd 7 is effectively the top "point" of the motif, so you are joining at the "northwest" point instead of the "western" point.

**Rnd 7:** sl st across next htr, 2htr, miss next htr, 4ch, 1dc into 4ch sp, 3dc, 1dc into 4ch sp, 2ch, sl st to centre of corresponding 4ch of previous motif, miss next htr, 2htr, 2ch, sl st to centre of corresponding 4ch of previous motif.

Continue round as normal, joining to motif below in normal way.

Join next two motifs in normal way, then join final motif of round to motif to its left and below as normal, but joining to first motif of round at the "northeast" point of star.

Weave in all ends and block lightly to shape.

### Filling
To fill in the diamonds between each motif, using 3.5 mm crochet hook and yarn A, ch5, join with a sl st to join rnd.

**Rnd 1:** ch1, work 16dc into ring, join rnd with sl st. **Joining rnd:** (work anticlockwise round the hole to be filled, slipstitching where indicated to each of 4 motifs that comprise the hole in turn.) 1ch, dc in first dc, *6ch, sl st into one of the joining slipped stitches between two motifs, 6ch, miss next dc in ring, dc into next dc, 4ch, sl st to centre stitch of motif comprising next side of diamond, 5ch, miss next dc in ring, dc into next dc; 6ch, sl st into one of the joining slipped stitches in between two motifs, 6ch, miss next dc in ring, dc into next dc, 5ch, sl st to centre stitch of motif comprising next side of diamond, 4ch, miss next dc in ring, dc into next dc; rep from * to end of rnd, sl st to first ch to join. Fasten off yarn.

Repeat for every diamond to be filled.

### Hem
Work the same as with the diamonds to joining rnd.
**Joining rnd:** (work anticlockwise round the hole to be filled, slipstitching where indicated to each of 2 motifs that comprise the hole in turn.) 6ch, sl st into 4ch of right motif, 6ch, miss next dc in ring, dc into next dc, 4ch, sl st to centre stitch of motif comprising side of diamond, 5ch, miss next dc in ring, dc into next dc, 6ch, sl st into next joining slipped stitch between two motifs, 6ch, miss next dc in ring, dc into next dc, 4ch, sl st to centre stitch of left motif comprising next side of diamond, 5ch, miss next dc in ring, dc into next dc, 6ch sl st into next 4ch of right motif, 6ch, miss next dc in ring, dc in next dc. Fasten off yarn.

Work the same round neck edge and each underarm.

### Finishing
Work a rnd of dc evenly all round neck edge.
Weave in all ends and block lightly to shape.

# Poolside Dress

Skill Level:
Intermediate

A delicate
design with
shout-out-loud
glamour, the
Ungaro dress,
opposite, is
worked with
appliqué
flowers.
Continuing
with the
openwork theme
is an easy-to-
wear bikini
cover-up,
right, which
will take you
from the beach
or pool to the
tiki bar.

## Poolside Dress
Claire Montgomerie

Crochet is the perfect technique for working up high-fashion mesh pieces, and although such see-through pieces are impractical for day-to-day wear, they make great beachwear. The open stitch creates a cool garment, which provides modesty without hiding that statement bikini.

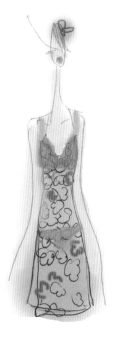

## YARN
4 [4:5:5] x 50 g (2 oz) balls of DMC Natura Just
    cotton, 100% cotton, 155 m (169 yds), in shade
    18, coral

## NOTIONS
4 mm (size 8) crochet hook
4.5 mm (size 7) crochet hook
Stitch marker
Tapestry needle

## MEASUREMENTS
Bust

| | | | |
|---|---|---|---|
| 81 | 86 | 91 | 96 cm |
| 32 | 34 | 36 | 38 in |

Actual size

| | | | |
|---|---|---|---|
| 81 | 86 | 91 | 96 cm |
| 32 | 34 | 36 | 38 in |

Length
90 cm
35½ in

## TENSION
17tr and 10 rows in trebles to measure 10 x 10 cm
(4 x 4 in) using 4 mm (size 8) hook or size to obtain
correct tension.

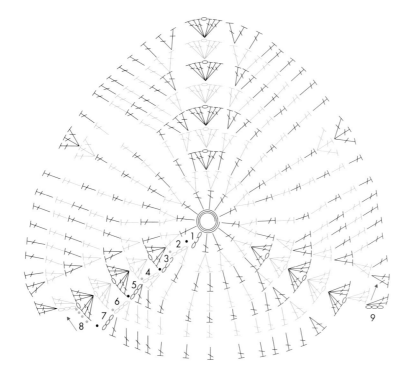

## PATTERN

**Bra Cups** Make 2.

**Rnd 1:** With 4 mm (size 8) hook, work 12tr into a magic ring.

**Rnd 2:** 3ch, work 2tr into each st around. Join with sl st to top of t-ch. *24tr.*

**Rnd 3:** 3ch, 6tr, (2tr, 1ch, 2tr) into next st, *7tr (2tr, 1ch, 2tr) into next st; rep from * once more, join rnd with sl st to top of t-ch. *33tr.*

**Rnd 4:** 3ch, tr into base of ch, 5tr, 2tr into next st, miss 2tr gp, (2tr, 2ch, 2tr) into ch sp, *miss 2tr gp, 2tr into next st, 5tr, 2tr into next st, miss 2tr gp, (2tr, 2ch, 2tr) into ch sp; rep from * once more, join rnd with sl st to top of t-ch.

**Rnd 5:** 3ch, tr into base of ch, 7tr, 2tr into next st, miss 2tr gp, (3tr, 2ch, 3tr) into ch sp, *miss 2 tr gp, 2tr into next st, 7tr, 2tr into next st, miss 2tr gp, (3tr, 2ch, 3tr) into ch sp; rep from * once more, join rnd with sl st to top of t-ch.

**Rnd 6:** 3ch, tr into base of ch, 9tr, 2tr into next st, miss 3tr gp, (3tr, 2ch, 3tr) into ch sp, *miss 3 tr gp, 2tr into next st, 9tr, 2tr into next st, miss 3tr gp, (3tr, 2ch, 3tr) into ch sp; rep from * once more, join rnd with sl st to top of t-ch.

**Rnd 7:** 3ch, tr into base of ch, 11tr, 2tr into next st, miss 3tr gp, (3tr, 2ch, 3tr) into ch sp, *miss 3 tr gp, 2tr into next st, 11tr, 2tr into next st, miss 3tr gp, (3tr, 2ch, 3tr) into ch sp; rep from * once more, join rnd with sl st to top of t-ch.

Turn and sl st back to ch sp. You will now just be working over top two sides of cup. Unworked side is bottom of cup.

**Rnd 8:** 3ch, 2tr into ch sp, miss next 3tr gp, 2tr into next st, 6tr, 3tr into next st, 6tr, 2tr into next st, miss next 3tr gp, (3tr, 2ch, 3tr) into ch sp, miss next 3tr gp, 2tr into next st, 6tr, 3tr into next st, 6tr, 2tr into next st, miss next 3tr gp, 3tr into ch sp. Turn.

**Rnd 9:** 3ch, 2tr into base of ch, miss next 3tr gp, 2tr into next st, 8tr, 3tr into next st, 8tr, 2tr into next st, miss 3tr gp, (3tr, 2ch, 3tr) into ch sp, miss next 3tr gp, 2tr into next st, 8tr, 3tr into next st, 8tr, 2tr into next st, miss 2tr, 3tr into last st.

Turn first size only.

Fasten off yarn.

## All Other Sizes

**Rnd 3:** 2ch, 2htr into base of ch, miss next 3tr gp, 2htr into next st, 10htr, 3htr into next st, 10htr, 2htr into next st, miss 3tr gp, (3tr, 2ch, 3tr) into ch sp, miss next 3tr gp, 2htr into next st, 10htr, 3htr into next st, 10htr, 2htr into next st, miss 2tr, 3htr into last st. Turn.

**Second size only:** Fasten off yarn.

## All Other Sizes

**Rnd 4:** 2ch, 2htr into base of ch, miss next 3htr gp, 2htr into next st, 12htr, 3htr into next st, 12htr, 2htr into next st, miss 3htr gp, (3tr, 2ch, 3tr) into ch sp, miss next 3htr gp, 2htr into next st, 12htr, 3htr into next st, 12htr, 2htr into next st, miss 2tr, 3htr into last st. Turn.

**Third size only:** Fasten off yarn.

## Largest Size Only

**Rnd 5:** 2ch, 2htr into base of ch, miss next 3htr gp, 2htr into next st, 14htr, 3htr into next st, 14htr, 2htr into next st, miss 3htr gp, (3tr, 2ch, 3tr) into ch sp, miss next 3htr gp, 2htr into next st, 14htr, 3htr into next st, 14htr, 2htr into next st, miss 2tr, 3htr into last st. Turn.

Fasten off yarn.

## Straps

Using 4 mm (size 8) hook, attach yarn to first tr of shell at top point of bra.

**Row 1–2:** 3ch, (3tr, 2ch, 3tr) into ch sp, tr into last tr of 3tr gp. Turn.

**Row 3–4:** 3ch, (2tr, 2ch, 2tr) into ch sp, tr into last st. Turn.

**Rows 5–7:** 3ch, (2tr, 1ch, 2tr) into ch sp, tr into last st. Turn.

**Row 8:** 3ch, (tr, 1ch, tr) into ch sp, tr into last st. Turn. Rep last row until strap measures approx 45 cm (17½ in) or desired length.

## Skirt

**Rnd 1:** Using 4 mm hook, ch 18, with RSF, work 4tr into end of right cup strap, ch18, with RSF, attach yarn to bottom of right cup and work 32[34:38:42]tr evenly along the cup, then work 32[34:38:42]tr along bottom of left cup, ch 18, with RSF, work 4tr into end of left cup strap, ch 18, join into rnd with sl st into first ch of rnd.

**Rnd 2:** ch 3 (counts as first tr), 1tr into each of next 17tr, 4tr from strap, 1tr into each of next 18ch, 64[68:76:84]tr along cups, 1tr into each of next 18ch, 4tr from strap, 1 tr into each ch to end of rnd, join rnd with sl st into t-ch. *144[148:156:164] tr.*

**Rnd 3:** 3ch, 1tr into each st to end of rnd, join rnd with sl st into t-ch.

**Rnd 4:** as last rnd.

**Rnd 5:** (6ch, miss 3tr, dc into next tr) to end of rnd, ending with dc into bottom of first ch.

**Rnd 6:** 6ch, dc into first ch sp, (6ch, dc into next ch sp) to end of rnd, do not join rnds from now on, but continue working in spirals, using a marker to mark start of rnd, move marker up each rnd.

Continue working in 6ch mesh

**Rnd 7–9:** Work 3 more rnds, ending last rnd with dc into ch sp.

**Rnd 10:** *(3tr, 2ch, 3tr) into next dc, dc into next ch sp, (6ch, dc into next ch sp) four times, rep from * to end of rnd.

**Rnd 11–16:** Work 6 further rnds in 6 ch mesh.

**Rnd 17:** (6ch, dc into next ch sp) twice, (3tr, 2ch, 3tr) into next dc, dc into next ch sp, *(6ch, dc into next ch sp) four times, (3tr, 2ch, 3tr) into next ch sp, dc into next ch sp; rep from * to end, finishing (6ch, dc into next ch sp) twice.

Change to 4.5 mm hook and work a further 6 rnds 6ch mesh.

**Rnd 24:** as rnd 10.

**Rnd 25–30:** Work a further 6 rnds 6 ch mesh.

**Rnd 31:** as rnd 11.

**Rnd 32–7:** Work a further 6 rnds mesh, but work 7ch sps instead of 6ch sps.

**Rnd 38:** *(3tr, 2ch, 3tr) into next dc, dc into next ch sp, (7ch, dc into next ch sp) four times, rep from * to end of rnd.

**Rnd 39–44:** Work a further 6 rnds 7 ch mesh

**Rnd 45:** *(3tr, 2ch, 3tr) into next dc, dc into next ch sp; rep from * to end of rnd, sl st to first dc of rnd. Fasten off yarn.

Weave in all ends and block into shape.

# Summer Mini Skirt

Skill Level:
Intermediate

The circular
pattern of
the Anna Sui
Spring/Summer
2011 shorts,
opposite, is
reinterpreted
in the crochet
miniskirt,
right, an
essential
summer piece
to wear
hippie-style
with fringing,
feathers
and a lacy
waistcoat.

## Summer Mini Skirt
Emma Varnam

Joining motifs is a fabulous way to create garments in crochet. The simple circles used here are a nod to the 1960s but still keep a modern feel. Attaching the motifs in rows also mean the skirt is easy to lengthen if you don't want to flash too much flesh! The skirt looks fabulous lined with a bright fabric or paired with some opaque tights for a more wintery garment.

## YARN
5[6] x 50 g (2 oz) skeins of Blue Sky Alpacas,
  50% alpaca, 50% silk, 133 m (146 yds) in
  shade 110, cream

## NOTIONS
2 mm (size 14) crochet hook
1 m (39½ in) of 1 cm (½ in) wide elastic

## MEASUREMENTS
To Fit Hips

| | |
|---|---|
| 76–81 | 86–91 cm |
| 30–32 | 34–36 in |

Finished Hips

| | |
|---|---|
| 84 | 98 cm |
| 33 | 38.5 in |

Length

| | |
|---|---|
| 33 | 35 cm |
| 13 | 13.75 in |

## TENSION/GAUGE
Each motif is 5.5 cm (2¼ in) in diameter.
Work 25st and 6 rows in tr tr st to measure 10 x 10
cm (4 x 4 in) using 2 mm (size 14) needles, or size
required to obtain tension.

## SPECIAL INSTRUCTIONS
The bottom half of the skirt is made from 3 rows of
circular motifs. These are joined together as you make
each motif.
For each row there are 14 [16] motifs.

**Note:** You can make the skirt longer by adding rows
of circular motifs or trtr rows.

## PATTERN
### Basic Motif
With 2 mm (size 14) hook, 6ch, sl st into 1st ch to form a ring.

**Rnd 1:** 1ch, 17dc into ring, sl st into 1st ch. *18 sts.*
**Rnd 2:** 6ch (miss 2dc, 1dc into next dc, 5 ch) 5 times, ss into 1st ch.
**Rnd 3:** sl st into 1st sp, 5ch, 7trtr into same sp, (8trtr into next sp) 5 times, sl st into 5th ch.
**Rnd 4:** 1ch, 1 dc into every trtr, sl st into 1st ch. *48 sts.* Fasten off.

### Second Motif of First Row
**Rnd 1–3:** Complete as for 1st until rnd 4.
**Rnd 4:** 1ch, 1 dc into 8 trtr, 2ch, sl st into 40th trtr of first motif, 2ch, sl st back into last dc of 2nd motif, 1dc into next 8trtr, 2ch, st st into 32nd trtr of first motif, 2ch, sl st back into last dc of 2nd motif, 1dc into rem trtr, st st into 1st ch. Fasten off.

Continue to add circular motifs until 13[15] motifs have been joined.

### Final Motif of First Row
**Rnd 1–3:** Complete as or 1st until rnd 4.
**Rnd 4:** 1ch, 1 dc into 8trtr, 2ch, sl st into 40th trtr of 13th[15th] motif, 2ch, sl st back into last dc of last motif, 1dc into next 8trtr, 2ch, st st into 32nd trtr of 13th[15th] motif, 2 ch, sl st back into last dc of last motif, 1dc into next 16trtr, 2ch, st st into 16 nd trtr of first motif, 2ch, sl st back into last dc of last motif, 1dc into next 8trtr, 2ch, st st into 8th trtr of first motif, 1dc into rem trtr, st st into 1st ch. Fasten off.

### First Motif of Second and Third Rows
**Rnd 1–3:** Complete as or 1st until rnd 4.
**Rnd 4:** 1ch, 1dc into 4trtr, 2ch, sl st into 28th trtr of a motif on the first row, 2ch, sl st back into last dc of 1st motif, 1 dc into next 40trtr, 2ch, st st into 20th trtr of motif on the first row, 2ch, sl st back into last dc of 1st motif, 1dc into rem trtr, st st into 1st ch. Fasten off.

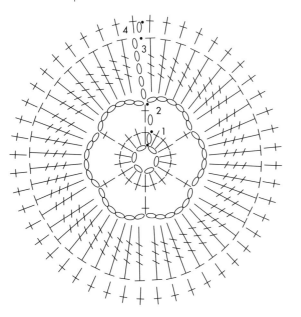

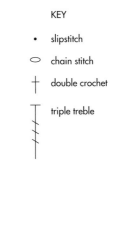

KEY

- • slipstitch
- ⌒ chain stitch
- † double crochet
- ⌶ triple treble

## Second Motif of Second and Third Rows

**Rnd 1–3:** Complete as or 1st until rnd 4.

**Rnd 4:** 1ch, 1dc into 4 trtr, 2ch, sl st into 28th trtr of a motif on the first row, 2ch, sl st back into last dc of 2nd motif, 1dc into 4trtr, 2ch, sl st into 40th trtr of first motif, 2ch, sl st back into last dc of 2nd motif, 1dc into next 8trtr, 2ch, st st into 32nd trtr of first motif, 2ch, sl st back into last dc of 2nd motif, 1dc into 28trtr, st st st st into 20th trtr of motif on the first row, 1dc into rem trtr, st st into 1st ch. Fasten off.

Continue to add circular motifs until 13[15] motifs have been joined.

## Final Motif of Second and Third Rows

**Rnd 1–3:** Complete as or 1st until rnd 4.

**Rnd 4:** 1ch, 1dc into 4 trtr, 2ch, sl st into 28th trtr of a motif on the first row, 2ch, sl st back into last dc of final motif, 1dc into 4trtr, 2ch, sl st into 40th trtr of 13th[15th] motif, 2ch, sl st back into last dc of final motif, 1dc into next 8trtr, 2ch, st st into 32nd trtr of 13th[15th] motif, 2ch, sl st back into last dc of final motif, 1dc into next 16trtr, 2ch, st st into 16th trtr of first motif, 2ch, sl st back into last dc of final motif, 1dc into next 8trtr, 2ch, st st into 8th trtr of first motif, 1dc into 4trtr, sl st into 20th trtr of a motif on the first row, 2ch, sl st back into last dc of final motif, st st into 1st ch.
Fasten off.

Once you have joined the final motif in the 3rd row, do not fasten off but join the edges together.

**Edge Row:** 1ch, 1dc in next 2 dc of motif, 10ch, sl st in join between 8th and 40th dc, 3 ch, sl st in 3rd ch from dc, 6 ch, *dc in top 4dc of next motif, 10ch, sl st in join between 8th and 40th dc, 3ch, sl st in 3rd ch from dc, 6ch, rep from * to last motif, 2dc in top of last motif, sl st in ch.

## Treble Treble Rows

Work in rounds.

**Row 1:** 5ch (forms first trtr), 1trtr in next dc, * 1trtr in next 12ch sts, 1trtr, in next 4 dc, rep from, rep from * 12[13] times, 1trtr in next 12ch sts, 1trtr in next 2dc. sl st into 5th ch. *224[256] sts.*

**Row 2:** 5ch (forms first trtr), 1trtr in each trtr, sl st into 5th ch. *224[256] sts.*

Rep row 2 until 6[7]trtr rows have been worked.

## Waistband

Work in rounds.

**Row1:** 1ch, dc in each trtr st, sl st into ch st.

**Row 2:** 4ch (forms first dtr), dtr in each dc to end, stl st into 4ch. *224[256] sts.*

**Rows 3–5:** Rep row 2.

Fold the waist band over in half, making sure you leave a gap in order to thread the elastic through. Attach the last row of waistband to the dc row at the beg of waist band with sl st.

### Hem Edge

With RS facing and using 2 mm (size14) crochet hook, join yarn to the base of one of the motifs of the first row. (Try to make sure this is at the back and corresponds to the joining chains on the waistband rows.)

**Edge row:** 1ch, 1dc in next 2 dc of motif, 10ch, sl st in join between 8th and 40th dc, 3ch, sl st in 3rd ch from dc, 6ch, *dc in top 4dc of next motif, 10ch, sl st in join between 8th and 40th dc, 3ch, sl st in 3rd ch from dc, 6ch, rep from * to last motif, 2 dc in top of last motif, sl st in ch.

**Triple Treble row:** 5ch (forms first trtr), 1trtr in next dc, * 1trtr in next 12ch sts, 1trtr, in next 4 dc, rep from, rep from * 12[13] times, 1trtr in next 12 ch sts, 1trtr in next 2dc. sl st into 5th ch, turn. *224[256] sts.*

**Next row (WS):** 4ch, miss 3[2] trtr, dc into next tr, *4ch, miss 2trtr, dc into next tr, rep from * to end. Turn.

**Next row (RS):** *5dc into ch sp, sl st into dc, rep from * to end.

Fasten off. Weave in ends.

### Finishing

Using the ball band as a guide, block the work to make sure the circular motifs are set.

Cut a length of 1 cm (½ in) elastic to fit around your waist with an overlap. Thread the elastic through the waistband and sew two ends securely tog through both thicknesses. Sl st the gap at the waistband opening. Fasten off and weave in ends.

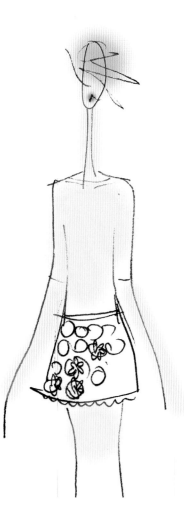

Skill Level:
Intermediate

Unlike the
simple Granny-
Square Cowl on
pages 14-7,
which utilizes
conventional
shades,
this skirt
is worked
in a more
contemporary,
monochrome
colour palette
of greys. The
grading of
colours in one
huge square is
interesting
and striking;
you could also
use varying
shades of
pretty pastel
nude hues to
great effect.

## Monochrome Granny-Square Skirt

Claire Montgomerie

Granny squares
are one of the most
traditional and
recognizable motifs
used in crochet.
Traditionally used for
cushions and throws,
many high-profile
designers have used
this familiar technique
in new and interesting
ways to create
fashionable garments.
Here, the on-trend
pencil skirt silhouette
works brilliantly
with the geometric
granny stitch.

## YARN

1 x 50 g (2 oz) ball of Debbie Bliss Rialto DK, 100%
extra fine merino wool, 105 m (114 yds) in shade
01, white (yarn A)

3 x 50 g (2 oz) balls of Debbie Bliss Rialto DK, 100%
extra fine merino wool, 105 m (114 yds) in shade
04, grey (yarn B)

3[4:5:6] x 50 g (2 oz) balls of Debbie Bliss Rialto DK,
100% extra fine merino wool, 105 m (114 yds) in
shade 33, charcoal (yarn C)

## NOTIONS

3.5 mm (size 9) crochet hook
4 mm (size 8) crochet hook
10 small buttons, approximately 1 cm (½ in) diameter
Tapestry needle
Sewing needle and thread to match buttons

## MEASUREMENTS

**Note:** should be worn with slight negative ease
to allow for the pencil skirt silhouette.

Waist

| 64 | 66 | 71 | 76 cm |
|----|----|----|-------|
| 25 | 26 | 28 | 30 in |

Hips

| 83 | 87 | 92 | 97 cm |
|-----|----|----|-------|
| 32½ | 34 | 36 | 38 in |

Length

| 55 | 55 | 55 | 55 cm |
|-----|-----|-----|--------|
| 21½ | 21½ | 21½ | 21½ in |

## TENSION/GAUGE

Approximately 4 patt reps and 8.5 rows to 10 x 10
cm (4 x 4 in) over granny pattern (one pattern rep is
3tr, 1ch) using 4 mm (size 8) hook, or size required
to obtain correct tension.

18dc and 25rows to 10 cm (4 in) in dc using 3.5 mm
(size 9) hook or size required to obtain correct tension.

Christopher Kane's granny-square skirt from
Autumn/Winter 2011, above, features a shiny
metallic wool to give a slick finish. The
granny square motif is even printed onto the
leather jacket, elevating this humble pattern
to high-fashion status.

The granny-square centre is worked from lighter colours outwards, with the deep charcoal colour gradually dominating the front and merging into the solid-coloured back.

## PATTERN
### Front
All Sizes.

Using 4 mm (size 8) hook and yarn A, ch4, join to first ch with a sl st to form ring.

**Rnd 1:** ch3 (counts as 1st tr), 2tr in ring, ch3, (3tr in ring, ch3) three times, join rnd with sl st to top of first ch. Break off yarn.

**Rnd 2:** Join yarn B to any 3-ch corner sp, ch3 (counts as 1st tr), work (2tr, ch3, 3tr) all in same 3-ch sp, ch 1, *work (3tr, ch3, 3tr) all in next 3-ch sp, ch1; rep from * twice more, join rnd with sl st to top of first ch. Break off yarn.

**Rnd 3:** Join yarn A to any 3-ch corner sp ch3, work (2tr, ch3, 3tr) all in same sp for corner, ch 1, 3tr in next 1-ch sp, ch1, *work (3tr, ch3, 3tr) all in next 3-ch sp for corner, ch 1, 3tr in next 1-ch sp, ch1; rep from * around, join rnd with sl st to top of first ch. Break off yarn.

**Rnd 4:** Join yarn B to any 3-ch corner sp, ch3, work (2tr, ch3, 3tr) in same sp, ch1, (3tr in next 1-ch sp, ch1) twice, *work (3tr, ch3, 3tr) in next corner sp, ch1, (3tr in next 1-ch sp, ch1) twice; rep from * around, join rnd with sl st to top of first ch, sl st to next 3-ch sp.

**Rnd 5:** ch3, work (2tr, ch 3, 3tr) in same sp, ch1, (3tr in next 1-ch sp, ch1) three times, *work (3tr, ch 3, 3tr) in next corner sp, ch1, (3tr in next 1-ch sp, ch1) three times; rep from * around, join rnd with sl st to top of first ch, sl st to next 3-ch sp.

**Rnd 6:** ch 3, work (2tr, ch 3, 3tr) in same sp, ch1, (3tr in next 1-ch sp, ch1) four times, *work (3tr, ch 3, 3tr) in next corner sp, ch1, (3tr in next 1-ch sp, ch1) four times; rep from * around, join rnd with sl st to top of first ch, sl st to next 3-ch sp. Break off yarn.

**Rnd 7:** Join yarn C to any 3ch corner sp, ch3, work (2tr, ch3, 3tr) in same sp, ch1, (3tr in next 1-ch sp, ch1) to next corner sp, *work (3tr, ch3, 3tr) in next corner sp, ch1, (3tr in next 1-ch sp, ch1) to next corner sp; rep from * around, join rnd with sl st to top of first ch. Break off yarn.

**Rnd 8:** Join yarn B to any 3-ch corner sp, rep last rnd once more, sl st to next 3-ch sp.

**Rnd 9:** ch 3, work (2tr, ch 3, 3tr) in same sp, ch1, (3tr in next 1-ch sp, ch1) to next corner sp, *work (3tr, ch 3, 3tr) in next corner sp, ch1, (3tr in next 1-ch sp, ch1) to next corner sp; rep from * around, join rnd with sl st to top of first ch.
Break off yarn.

Repeat last round changing colours for the rounds in the following sequence:
**Rnd 10:** yarn C
**Rnds 11–12:** yarn B
**Rnd 13:** yarn C
**Rnd 14:** yarn B
**Rnds 15–16:** yarn C
**Rnd 17:** yarn B
**Rnds 18–20:** yarn C
**Rnd 21:** yarn B
**Rnd 22:** yarn C
sl st to next corner sp. Do not fasten off.

## Back
Turn, continue with yarn C and begin to work in rows as follows:
**Row 1:** 3ch, 2tr into corner sp, (1ch, 3tr into next ch sp) to end of row. Turn.
**Row 2:** 4ch, (3tr into next ch sp, 1ch) to end of row, ending with tr into third of 3tr cluster. Turn.
**Row 3:** 3ch, 2tr into next sp, (1ch, 3tr into next ch sp) to end of row. Turn.
Rep rows 2 and 3 6[7:8:9] further times.
Fasten off yarn.

With WSF, fasten yarn C to corner space of corner of opposite side of fabric, and continue work to create a long strip as follows:
**Row 1:** 3ch, 2tr into corner sp, (1ch, 3tr into next ch sp) to end of row. Turn
**Row 2:** 4ch, (3tr into next ch sp, 1ch) to end of row, ending with tr into third of 3tr cluster. Turn.
**Row 3:** 3ch, 2tr into next sp, (1ch, 3tr into next ch sp) to end of row. Turn.
Rep rows 2 and 3 5[6:7:8] further times, then work a row 2 once more.

Work a final row 3, joining skirt at back centre hem as follows. Fold skirt so that the short sides meet at centre back hem:
**Next row:** 3ch, 2tr into next sp, (1ch, 3tr into next ch sp) 7 times, *sl st to corresponding ch sp of opposite seam edge of skirt, 3tr into next ch sp; rep from * to end of row.
Fasten off yarn and weave in ends.
Block piece lightly to shape.

## Hem Edging
Using yarn C and 4 mm (size 6) hook, work a multiple of 6, plus 1 dc evenly around closed, hem edge of skirt. sl st to join rnd.

Work pointed scallop edge onto this dc rnd as follows: ch1, miss 2dc, [3tr, 3ch, 3tr] into next dc, miss 2 dc, *1dc into next st, miss 2dc, (3tr, 3ch, 3tr) into next dc, miss 2dc; rep from * to end of rnd, sl st to first ch to join rnd. Fasten off yarn.

## Waistband

Using 3.5 mm (size 9) hook and yarn B, work 140[150:160:170] dc evenly along the top edge of the skirt.

**Row 2:** ch 1, work in dc to end of row.

**Row 3:** ch 1, (12[13:14:15]dc, dec 1 dc over next 2 sts) to end of rnd. 130(140:150:160) dc.

**Rows 4–5:** ch1, work in dc to end of row.

**Row 6:** ch1, (11[12:13:14]dc, dec 1 dc over next 2 sts) to end of rnd. 120(130:140:150) dc.

**Rows 7–8:** ch1, work in dc to end of row.

**Row 9:** ch1, (10[11:12:13] dc, dec 1 dc over next 2 sts) to end of rnd. 110(120:130:140) dc.

**Row 10:** ch1, work in dc to end of row.

## Button Band

Using 3.5 mm (size 9) hook and yarn B, work 41dc down right back opening. Turn and work 2 further rows straight in dc on these sts.
Fasten off yarn.

Attach yarn to top of left side of back opening and work 41dc evenly down the left side.
Turn and work one further row straight in dc, turn.

**Next row:** ch1, (does not count as st) dc into first dc, (3ch, miss next st, 3dc) to end of row. 10 button loops made. Fasten off yarn.

## Finishing

Weave in ends and block edges lightly.
Sew 10 buttons to right button band, in corresponding positions to button loops.

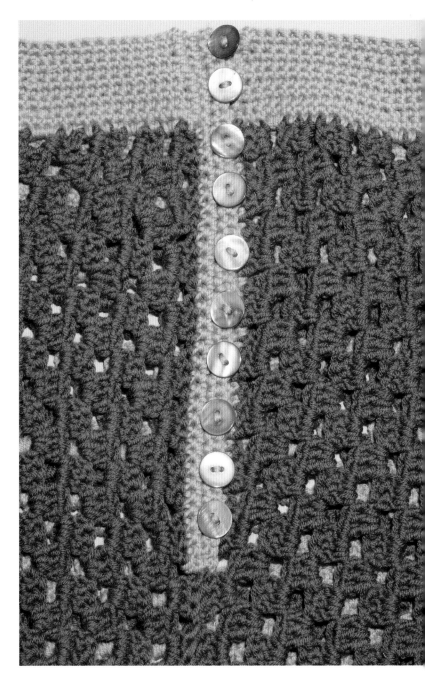

Skill Level:
Intermediate

## Beach Shorts

Emma Varnam

Go from beach to bar in these nautical summer shorts. Paired with a stripy Breton top for a Riviera style, they look tidy and chic while also being relaxed enough for yachting or other seaside sports. They use a practical cotton and a pretty pointelle-style stitch.

## YARN

4[5] x 50 g (2 oz) balls of DMC Natura Just cotton, 100% cotton, 155 m (170 yds) in shade 01, Ibiza (MC)

1 x 50 g (2 oz) ball of DMC Natura Just cotton, 100% cotton, 155 m (170 yds) in shade 28, zaphire (CC)

## NOTIONS

3 mm (size 11) crochet hook
1 m (39½ in) of 2.5 cm (1 in) wide elastic

## MEASUREMENTS

Hips

| | |
|---|---|
| 76–81 | 86–91 cm |
| 30–32 | 34–36 in |

Length

| | |
|---|---|
| 30 | 33 cm |
| 11¾ | 13 in |

## TENSION/GAUGE

Work 8.5cl and 14 rows in palm leaf pattern to measure 10 x 10 cm (4 x 4 in) using 3 mm (size 11) hook, or size required to obtain tension.

## SPECIAL INSTRUCTIONS

### Crab Stitch:

**Rnd 1:** Work evenly round edge in dc. sl st to join edge. Do NOT turn work.
**Rnd 2:** Work one row in reverse dc, working first st into last dc of last round, then each following stitch into next dc to the RIGHT of the last rather than the left.

Shorts make it onto the catwalk every time there's a cruisewear collection, as they are favourites for resort holidays. Above a model walks down the runway during the Triton fashion show in Sao Paulo, Brazil, wearing a drawstring pair and opposite Kourtney Kardashian is shown in a feminine lacy style. Many fashion and swimwear brands, such as Melissa Odabash and Tory Burch, make crochet beach shorts in short and long lengths.

## PATTERN
### Left Front

With 3 mm (size 11) hook using MC, 55[64] ch. Turn.

**Row 1:** dc in 4th ch from hook, * 2ch, miss next 2ch, 1dc in next ch, rep from * to end. Turn.

**Row 2:** 3ch (counts as 1st tr) 1tr into first dc, *3tr into next dc, rep from * to end, 2tr into first of the 3ch. Turn. *18[21] cl.*

**Row 3:** 3ch, 1dc into 2nd tr of the first 3tr group, * 2ch, 1dc into 2nd tr of next 3tr group, rep from * to end working last dc into 3rd of the 3ch. Turn.
Rows 2 and 3 form the Palm Leaf pattern.

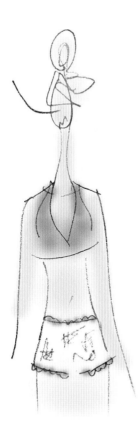

**Row 4 (inc row):** 3ch (counts as 1st tr) 1tr into first dc, *3tr into next dc, rep from * to end, 5tr into first of the 3ch. Turn. *19[22] cl.*

**Row 5:** 3ch, 1dc nto 2nd tr of the first 3tr group, * 2ch, 1 dc into 2nd tr of next 3tr group, rep from * to end working last dc into 3rd of the 3ch. Turn.

**Rows 6–7:** Rep rows 2–3. *19[22] cl.*

**Row 8:** 3ch (counts as 1st tr) 1tr into first dc, *3tr into next dc, rep from * to end, 5tr into first of the 3 ch. Turn. *20[23] cl.*

**Row 9:** 3ch, 1dc into 4th tr of the first 5tr group, * 2ch, 1dc into 2nd tr of next 3tr group, rep from * to end working last dc into 3rd of the 3ch. Turn.

**Row 10:** sl st 6 sts, dc in next st, 3ch (counts as 1st tr), 1tr into same dc, *3tr into next dc, rep from * to end, 2tr into first of the 3ch. Turn. *18[21] cl.*

**Row 11–27:** Cont to work pattern straight until you have completed 27 rows increasing as set at side seam at the end of 12th, 16th and 20th row. *21[24] cl.*

**Row 28:** 3ch (counts as 1st tr) 1tr into first dc, *3tr into next dc, rep from * to last two clusters, 1tr into next dc, 1tr in first of the 3ch. Turn.

**Row 29:** 3ch, 1dc into 2nd tr of the first 3tr group, * 2ch, 1dc into 2nd tr of next 3tr group, rep from * to end working last dc into 3rd of the 3ch, turn. *20[23] cl.*

**Row 30–36[38]:** Cont to work pattern straight until you have completed 36[38] rows. Fasten off.

### Right Front

With 3 mm (size11) hook and using MC, 55[64] ch. Turn.

**Row 1:** dc in 4th ch from hook, * 2ch, miss next 2 ch, 1 dc in next ch, rep from * to end. Turn.

**Row 2:** 3ch (counts as 1st tr) 1tr into first dc, *3tr into next dc, rep from * to end, 2tr into first of the 3ch. Turn. *18[21] cl.*

**Row 3:** 3ch, 1dc into 2nd tr of the first 3tr group, * 2ch, 1dc into 2nd tr of next 3tr group, rep from * to end working last dc into 3rd of the 3ch. Turn.
Rows 2 and 3 form the pattern.

**Row 4 (inc row):** 3ch (counts as 1st tr) 4tr into first dc, *3tr into next dc, rep from * to end, 2tr into first of the 3ch. Turn. *19[22] cl.*

**Row 5:** 3ch, 1 dc into 2nd tr of the first 3tr group, *2ch, 1 dc into 2nd tr of next 3tr group, rep from* to end working last dc into 3rd of the 3ch. Turn.

**Rows 6–7:** Rep rows 2–3. *19[22] cl.*

**Row 8:** 3ch (counts as 1st tr) 4tr into first dc, *3tr into next dc, rep from * to end, 2tr into first of the 3ch. Turn. *20[23] cl.*

**Row 9:** sl st 6 sts, 1dc into 2nd tr of next 3tr group, *2ch, 1 dc into 2nd tr of next 3tr group, rep from * to end working last dc into 3rd of the 3ch. Turn.

**Row 10:** 3ch (counts as 1st tr) 1tr into first dc, *3tr into next dc, rep from * to end, 2tr into the last dc. Turn. *18[21] cl.*

**Row 11–27:** Cont to work patt straight until you have completed 27 rows increasing as set at side seam at the end of 12th, 16th and 20th row. *21[24] cl.*

**Row 28:** 3ch (counts as 1st tr) 1tr into next dc, *3tr into next dc, rep from * to last to end, 2tr in first of the 3ch. Turn.

**Row 29:** 3ch, 1dc into 2nd tr of the first 3tr group, * 2ch, 1dc into 2nd tr of next 3tr group, rep from * to end working last dc, miss dc, dc into 3rd of the 3ch. Turn. *20[23] cl.*

**Row 30–36[38]:** Cont to work patt straight until you have completed 36[38] rows. Fasten off.

## Left Back

With 3 mm (size 11) hook and using MC, 70[79]ch. Turn.

**Row 1:** dc in 4th ch from hook, * 2ch, miss next 2ch, 1dc in next ch, rep from * to end. Turn.

**Row 2:** 3ch (counts as 1st tr) 1tr into first dc, *3tr into next dc, rep from * to end, 2tr into first of the 3ch. Turn. *23[26] cl.*

**Row 3:** 3ch, 1dc into 2nd tr of the first 3tr group, * 2ch, 1dc into 2nd tr of next 3tr group, rep from * to end working last dc into 3rd of the 3ch. Turn. Rows 2 and 3 form the pattern.

**Row 4 (inc row):** 3ch (counts as 1st tr) 4tr into first dc, *3tr into next dc, rep from * to end, 2tr into first of the 3ch. Turn. *24[27] cl.*

**Row 5:** 3ch, 1dc into 2nd tr of the first 3tr group, * 2ch, 1dc into 2nd tr of next 3tr group, rep from * to end working last dc into 3rd of the 3ch. Turn.

**Rows 6–7:** Rep rows 2–3. *24[27] cl.*

**Row 8:** 3ch (counts as 1st tr) 4tr into first dc, *3tr into next dc, rep from * to end, 2tr into first of the 3ch. Turn. *25[28] cl.*

**Row 9:** sl st 12 sts, 1vdc into 2nd tr of next 3tr group, * 2ch, 1 dc into 2nd tr of next 3tr group, rep from * to end working last dc into 3rd of the 3ch. Turn.

**Row 10:** 3ch (counts as 1st tr) 1tr into first dc, *3tr into next dc, rep from * to end, 2tr into the last dc. Turn. *21[24] cl.*

**Row 11:** ch, 1dc into 2nd tr of the first 3tr group, * 2ch, 1dc into 2nd tr of next 3tr group, rep from * to end working last dc into 3rd of the 3ch. Turn.

**Row 12:** 3ch (counts as 1st tr) 4tr into first dc, *3tr into next dc, rep from * to last two clusters, 1tr into next dc, 1tr in first of the 3ch. Turn. *21[24] cl.*

**Row 13:** 3ch, 1 dc into 2nd tr of the first 3tr group, * 2ch, 1dc into 2nd tr of next 3tr group, rep from * to end working last dc into 3rd of the 3ch. Turn.

**Row 14:** 3ch (counts as 1st tr) 1tr into first dc, *3tr into next dc, rep from * to last two clusters, 1tr into next dc, 1tr in first of the 3ch. Turn. *20[23] cl.*

**Row 15–27:** Cont to work pattern straight until you have completed 27 rows increasing as set at side seam at the end of 16th and 20th row. *22[25]cl.*

**Row 28:** 3ch (counts as 1st tr) 1tr into next dc, *3tr into next dc, rep from * to last to end, 2tr in first of the 3ch. Turn.

**Row 29:** 3ch, 1dc into 2nd tr of the first 3tr group, *2ch, 1dc into 2nd tr of next 3tr group, rep from * to end working last dc, miss dc, dc into 3rd of the 3ch. Turn. *21[24] cl.*

**Row 30–36[38]:** Cont to work pattern straight until you have completed 36[38] rows. Fasten off.

## Right Back

With 3 mm (size11) hook and usign MC, 70[79] ch. Turn.

**Row 1:** dc in 4th ch from hook, * 2ch, miss next 2ch, 1dc in next ch, rep from * to end. Turn

**Row 2:** 3ch (counts as 1st tr) 1tr into first dc, *3tr into next dc, rep from * to end, 2 tr into first of the 3ch. Turn. *23[26]cl.*

**Row 3:** 3ch, 1dc into 2nd tr of the first 3tr group, *
2ch, 1dc into 2nd tr of next 3tr group, rep from *
to end working last dc into 3rd of the 3ch. Turn.
Rows 2 and 3 form the pattern.

**Row 4 (inc row):** 3ch (counts as 1st tr) 1tr into first dc,
*3tr into next dc, rep from * to end, 5tr into first of the
3ch. Turn. *24[27] cl.*

**Row 5:** 3ch, 1dc into 2nd tr of the first 3tr group,
*2ch, 1dc into 2nd tr of next 3tr group, rep from *
to end working last dc into 3rd of the 3ch. Turn.

**Rows 6–7:** Rep rows 2–3. *24[27] cl.*

**Row 8:** 3ch (counts as 1st tr) 1tr into first dc, *3tr into
next dc, rep from * to end, 5tr into first of the 3ch.
Turn. *25[28] cl.*

**Row 9:** 3ch, 1dc into 4th tr of the first 5tr group, *
2ch, 1dc into 2nd tr of next 3tr group, rep from *
to end working last dc into 3rd of the 3ch. Turn.

**Row 10:** sl st 12 sts, dc in next st, 3ch (counts as 1st
tr), 1tr into same dc, *3tr into next dc, rep from * to
end, 2tr into first of the 3ch. Turn. *21[24] cl.*

**Row 11:** 3ch, 1dc into 2nd tr of the first 3tr group, *
2ch, 1 dc into 2nd tr of next 3tr group, rep from * to
end working last dc into last dc. Turn.

**Row 12:** 3ch (counts as 1st tr) 1tr into next dc, *3tr
into next dc, rep from * to end, 5tr into first of the 3ch.
Turn. *21[24] cl.*

**Row 13:** 3ch, 1dc nto 4th tr of the first 5tr group, *
2ch, 1 dc into 2nd tr of next 3tr group, rep from * to
end working last dc into 3rd of the 3ch. Turn.

**Row 14:** 3ch (counts as 1st tr) 1tr into next dc, *3tr
into next dc, rep from * to end 2tr into first of the 3ch.
Turn. *20[23] cl.*

**Row 15–27:** Cont to work pattern straight until you
have completed 27 rows increasing as set at side
seam at the end of 16th and 20th row. *22[25] cl.*

**Row 28:** 3ch (counts as 1st tr) 1tr into first dc, *3tr into
next dc, rep from * to last two clusters, 1tr into next dc,
1tr in first of the 3ch. Turn. *21[24] cl.*

**Row 29:** 3ch, 1dc into 2nd tr of the first 3tr group, *
2ch, 1dc into 2nd tr of next 3tr group, rep from * to
end working last dc into 3rd of the 3ch. Turn.

**Row 30–36[38]:** Cont to work pattern straight until you
have completed 36[38] rows. Fasten off.

## Edging

With WS tog, join short inside leg seam of left and
right side.

**Left Leg:** Using 3 mm (size 10) hook and CC, with RS
facing and with bottom hem at the top, join yarn at
left side at row 4 and work 1 round evenly in dc. join
edge with sl st. DO NOT turn work, then work next
round in crab stitch, fasten off yarn.

**Right Leg:** Repeat as for left leg.

With WS facing, join side seams of each leg, beg at
the top of crab stitch hem edging.

Turn right leg right side out. Keep left leg, wrong side
out. Place left leg inside right leg and pin along gusset
edge making sure seams match. Join gusset seam
together securely. Weave in all ends.

## Waistband

Work in rounds around the top of the shorts.
With WS facing at the centre of the back attach yarn
1ch, dc in each st around the top of the shorts, approx
244[274] sts, sl st into ch.

**Rows 1–4:** 4ch, 1dtr in each dc to end, sl st in 4th ch.

Fold the waistband over in half, making sure you leave
a gap in order to thread the elastic through. Attach
the last row of waistband to the dc row at the beg of
waist band with sl st. Cut a length of 2.5 cm (1 in)
elastic to fit around your waist with an overlap. Thread
the elastic through the waistband and sew two ends
securely tog through both thicknesses. Sl st the gap at
the waistband opening. Fasten off and weave in ends.

## I-Cord Tie

Using 3 mm and MC ch150, sl st back along the
length by placing the hook into the loop on the rev side
of the ch. Fasten off, weave in ends.

Thread the i-cord through the centre 14sts of the
waistband. Knot the ends of the i-cord, tie in a bow.

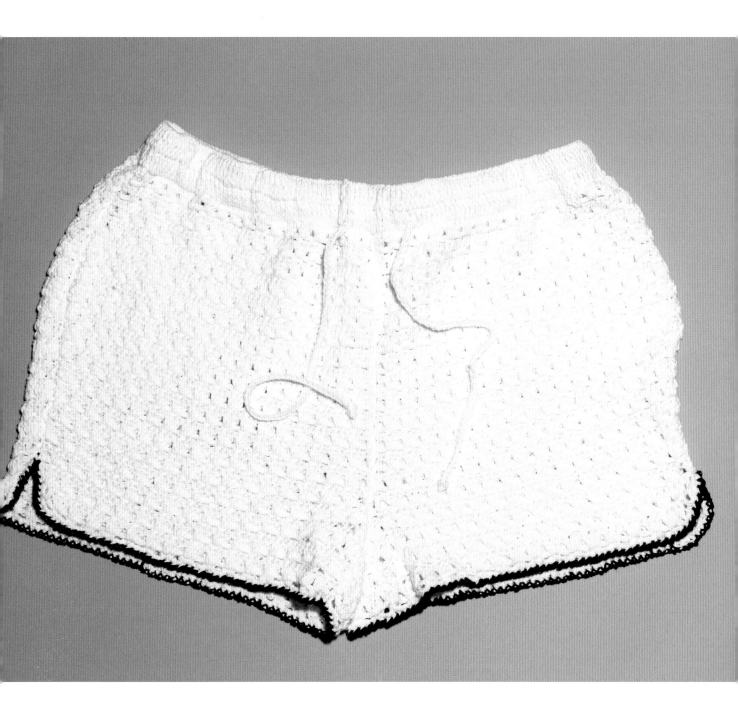

Hairpin Lace Top

Janis Waistcoat

Turqoise Beaded Top

Pineapple Lace Top

tops &
jumpers

Cornflower Fringe Top

Chunky Cabled Cardigan

Cabled Crochet Sweater

Colour Block Sweater

# Janis Waistcoat

Claire Montgomerie

Cute little lace and crocheted waistcoats are a summer favourite, so this simple yet decorative vest was developed as an accompaniment to many warm-weather outfits. Layer it over a maxi-dress for relaxed evening style or wear it with a vest, cut-off denim shorts and wellies to outdoor music festivals.

## Janis Waistcoat

Skill Level: Basic

The perfect boho piece, this light-weight waist-coat can be worn with a pretty frock for a feminine style or with shorts and wellies as an outdoor casual look – á la Sienna Miller, opposite.

## YARN
3[3:3:4] x 50 g (2 oz) skeins of Blue Sky Alpacas,
   50% alpaca, 50% silk, 133 m (146 yds), in shade
   110, natural

## NOTIONS
4 mm (size 8) crochet hook
Tapestry needle

## MEASUREMENTS
**Note:** Waistcoat does not close/meet at centre front.

Bust

| 76–81 | 86–91 | 96–101 | 106–111 cm |
|-------|-------|--------|------------|
| 30–32 | 34–36 | 38–40  | 42–44 in   |

Actual Size

| 86 | 97 | 107 | 117 cm |
|----|----|-----|--------|
| 33 | 38 | 42  | 46 in  |

Length

| 40 | 43 | 44 | 45 cm |
|----|----|----|-------|
| 16 | 17 | 17 | 18 in |

## TENSION/GAUGE
4 pattern repeats = 10.5 cm (4¼ in) and 7.5 rows
= 10 cm (4 in) using 4 mm (size 8) hook, or size
required to obtain tension.

## SPECIAL INSTRUCTIONS
**V st:** (tr, 2ch, tr) into indicated stitch.
**Pattern repeat:** (1V st into V st, 1tr into tr) to end.
**V stitch decrease (worked over 2 rows).**
**VstdecR1:** (if at start of row), 3ch, tr in 2ch-sp, tr in tr (if
at end of row, worked over last patt rep) 1tr into ch sp
of V st, 1tr into last tr.
**VstdecR2:** (if at start of row), 3ch, miss 1tr, 1tr in next tr
(if at end of row, worked over last 3tr) yrh, insert hk in
1st tr, yrh, draw yarn through, yrh, draw yarn through
2lps, miss one tr, yrh, insert hk in next tr, yrh, draw yarn
through, yrh, draw yarn through 2lps, yrn, draw yarn
through 3lps on hook.

Turning chain counts as tr unless otherwise stated.

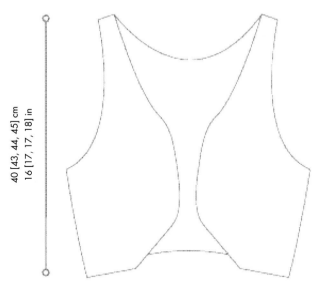

40 [43, 44, 45] cm
16 [17, 17, 18] in

## PATTERN
### Body

Using 4 mm (size 6) hook, ch112[128:144:156].

**Row 1:** Work 1 V st into 5th ch from hook, miss 1ch, 1tr into next ch, *miss 1ch, 1 V st into next ch, miss 1ch, 1 tr into next ch, rep from * to end. Turn. *27[31:35:38] patt reps + 1 tr.*

**Row 2:** 3ch, (1V st into V st, 1tr into tr) to end.

**Row 3:** 3ch, 1tr into base of chain, patt to end, ending with 2tr in t-ch, turn. *27[31:35:38] patt reps +3tr.*

**Row 4:** 3ch, 1 V st into base of ch, tr into tr, patt to last 2tr, 1tr plus 1 V st into next tr, 1tr into t-ch. Turn. *29[33:37:40] patt reps + 1tr.*

Rep last 2 increase rows until there are 33[37:41:44] patt reps + 1tr, then work straight in pattern until piece measures approx 16 cm (6¼ in), approx 12 rows from ch edge, or desired length to armhole.

With RSF, counting from right to left, place a stitch marker in the 2ch sp of V st 10[11:12:14].

## Right Front Neck and Armhole

**Row 1(RS):** **3ch, work across 7[8:9:9] patt reps. Turn, leaving rem stitches unworked. *7[8:9:9] patt reps + 1tr.*

**Row 2:** VstdecR1 (*see special instructions*), patt across. Turn.

**Row 3:** VstdecR1, patt across to last 3tr, VstdecR2.

**Row 4:** patt across to last 3tr, VstdecR2. Turn. *5[6:7:7] patt reps + 1tr.*

**Row 5:** patt across.

**Row 6:** patt across to last V st, VstdecR1. Turn.

**Row 7:** VstdecR2, patt across to end. Turn. *4[5:6:6] patt reps + 1tr.*

## Large Size Only

**Row 8:** Rep row 2.

**Row 9:** Rep row 3. *5 patt reps + 1tr.*

## All Other Sizes

**Row 8:** patt across.

**Row 9:** VstdecR1, patt across, turn.

## All Sizes

**Row 10:** patt across, VstdecR2. *3[4:5:4] patt reps + 1tr.*

**Row 11:** patt across.

**Row 12:** Rep row 6.

**Row 13:** Rep row 7. *2[3:4:3] patt reps + 1tr.*

**Row 14:** patt across.

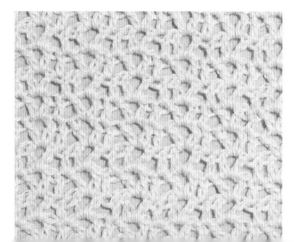

Continue as established decreasing on neck edge over 2 rows with one plain row in between decreases until 2[2:2:3] patt reps + 1tr remain. Then work straight till row count from beginning of armhole divide is 19[20:21:22] rows or desired length to shoulder. Fasten off yarn.**

## Left Front Neck and Armhole
Rejoin yarn to opposite edge of body, with WSF and rep as right front neckline and armhole between ** and **.

## Back
With RSF, and with sl st, join yarn in tr to the right of the marked 2ch-sp.
**Row 1(RS):** 3ch and work in patt along 15[17:19:18] patt reps. Turn.
**Row 2:** VstdecR1 in first patt rep, patt across to last patt rep, VstdecR1. Turn.
**Row 3:** VstdecR2, patt across to last 3tr, VstdecR2. Turn. *13[15:17:16] patt reps + 1tr.*
**Rows 4–6:** Work straight in patt.
**Row 7:** Rep row 2.
**Row 8:** Rep row 3. *11[13:15:14] patt reps + 1tr.*
Work straight till row count is one less than that of right and left sides and at the same time for 2 largest sizes, rep rows 2 and 3 for rows 12 and 13.
*11[13:15:14] patt reps + 1tr.*

## Shape Shoulder
**Next row:** 3ch, work across 2[2:2:3] patt reps. Fasten off yarn.
Rejoin yarn to opposite edge of back and work as first shoulder.

## Finishing
Block piece lightly to shape to open up stitch pattern. Sew together shoulder seams.
Work one row of dc evenly around edge of each armhole. Work one row of dc evenly around entire neck, front and bottom edging, being careful not to stretch or contract the fabric.

Weave in all ends and block lightly again.

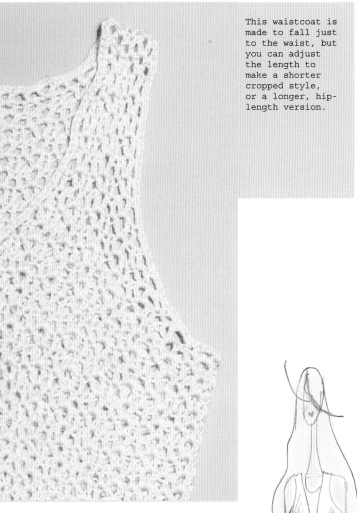

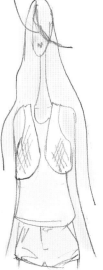

This waistcoat is made to fall just to the waist, but you can adjust the length to make a shorter cropped style, or a longer, hip-length version.

# Turquoise Beaded Top

Skill Level:
Intermediate

## Turquoise Beaded Top

Zoë Clements

The inspiration for this top came from the talented knitwear designer Mark Fast. His clothes are extremely innovative and modern, using flamboyant beading and interesting mesh and lace stitches. However, the garments also tend to be tight and revealing, which means that not every woman will want to wear them. This beautiful version uses strategically placed mesh and subtle yet gorgeous beading to create a classically contemporary garment that is flattering and comfortable to wear.

### YARN
6 [6:8:8] x 50 g (2 oz) balls of Sublime Egyptian cotton DK, 100% cotton, 105 m (115 yds) in shade 329

### NOTIONS
3.5 mm (size 9) crochet hook
Lockable stitch marker
Tapestry needle
440[460:480:500] blue size 6/0 seed beads
620[660:720:760] pink size 6/0 seed beads

### MEASUREMENTS

| Size | | | |
|------|------|------|------|
| S | M | L | XL |

| Bust | | | |
|------|------|------|------|
| 81.5 | 86.5 | 91.5 | 96.5 cm |
| 32 | 34 | 36 | 38 in |

| Length | | | |
|------|------|------|------|
| 53 | 53 | 56 | 56 cm |
| 21 | 21 | 22 | 22 in |

### TENSION/GAUGE
Work 24 rows and 20 sts in dc to measure 10 x 10 cm (4 x 4 in).

### SPECIAL INSTRUCTIONS
**Beaded Treble (btr):** yrh, insert hook into next st, yrh, pull up a loop, place bead, yrh, pull through 2 loops, place bead, yrh, pull through remaining 2 loops.

**Mesh Pattern:** 4ch (counts as 1tr, 1ch now and throughout), miss 1 tr, 1tr in next ch-sp, *1ch, 1tr in next ch-sp; rep from * across, 1tr in 3rd ch of t-ch, turn. Rep for pattern.

**Note:** Use the lockable stitch marker to help keep track of the ends of rounds in the body section, remembering to move it up each round as you go.

Nothing adds glitz to a crochet project like beads and sequins. These mesh mini-dresses from Mark Fast are lavishly embellished. For your projects, try experimenting with different sorts of beads – oblong or diamond shapes for example – or with sequins to create various effects. You can buy yarn with sequins already spun on, stitch beads in as you work, as directed here, or sew them onto the completed project as a finishing touch.

## PATTERN

### Neck

Thread yarn with 260[260:280:280] blue beads.
ch132[132:142:142].
Work a beaded treble into the 3rd ch from the
hook, and 1 btr in each ch across. sl st to 3rd ch
of t-ch to join.
Fasten off.

### Shoulders

Make 2.
Thread yarn with 130[130:140:140] pink beads.
ch67 (67: 77: 77).
Work a beaded treble into the 3rd ch from the hook,
and 1 beaded treble in each ch across. sl st to 3rd ch
of t-ch to join.
Fasten off.

### Joining Mesh

Take one shoulder circle and the neck circle and sl st
together, through one stitch in each circle only.
**Row 1:** sl st up 3 sts of the shoulder circle, 1ch, 1tr in
sl st join, 1ch, sl st to 3rd btr of neck circle.
**Row 2:** sl st up 3 sts of neck circle, 1ch, 1tr in ch-sp,
1ch, 1tr in ch-sp, 1ch, miss 2 btr of shoulder circle,
sl st to next btr.
**Row 3:** sl st up 3 sts of shoulder circle, *1ch, 1tr in
ch-sp; rep from * 2 more times, miss 2btr of neck
circle, sl st to next btr.
**Rows 4–5 [5: 6:6]:** rep rows 2 and 3 (ending
on a row 2 for sizes L & XL).
Fasten off.

Counting from the original sl st join, miss 64 sts
and rejoin yarn at the 65th btr. Repeat rows 1–5
[5:6:6] above.
Fasten off.

Repeat for the Back.

### Body

Re-attach yarn to the right shoulder circle, 8[8:10:10]
btr before the mesh starts.

ch4, miss 1 btr, 1tr in next btr, *1ch, miss 1btr, 1tr in
next st; rep from * across shoulder circle, working trs in
the ch-sps of the joining mesh, into sts of the neck circle,
into ch-sps of joining mesh and into sts of next 7 sts of
left shoulder circle, 1tr in next st. *76[76: 86: 86] sts.*

Work in Mesh Pattern until piece measures 18 cm
(7 in) from shoulder join.

### All Sizes

**Next row:** 1ch (does not count as a st now and
throughout), dc across, working 1dc in each ch-sp and
1dc in each st. Turn.
**Next row:** ch1, *1dc (blo), 1dc (flo); rep across. Turn.
*76[76:86:86] sts.*
**Next row:** ch1, *1dc(flo), 1dc(blo); rep across. Turn.
*76[76:86:86] sts.*
**Next row:** ch1, work in blo/flo patt as follows: 0[0:
5: 5]dc, *11dc, 2dc in next st, rep from * two more
times, 4dc, **2dc in next st, 11dc, rep from ** to last
0[0:5:5] dc, dc to end. Turn. *82[82:92:92] st.*
**Next row:** ch1, *1dc(blo), 1dc(flo); rep from * across.
Turn.
**Next row:** ch1, work in flo/blo patt as follows:
20[20:25:25] dc, 3dc in next st, 40dc, 3dc in next
st, 20[20:25:25]dc. Turn. *86[86:96:96] sts.*

### Sizes L & XL Only

ch1, work in flo/blo patt as follows: 20[20:25:25]
dc, 3dc in next st, 40dc, 3dc in next st,
20[20:25:25]dc. Turn.

Rep 4 more times. *86[86:96:96] sts.*
Fasten off. *86[96:106:116] sts.*

Repeat for the Back, but do not fasten off.

### Armhole
### Sizes M, L & XL Only

ch 10[10: 20].

## All Sizes
Join to first dc of the Front with a sl st, place marker (see pattern notes) and dc (blo/flo) in patt across.
Rep from * for joining the Back.
Work in patt in the round for 23 cm (9 in) from end of mesh pattern (working into the chains as appropriate for sizes M, L & XL).

## Waist Shaping
**Next rnd:** ch1, work in flo/blo patt as follows: 20[25:30:35]dc, dc3tog, 40dc, dc3tog, 20[25:30:35]dc.
**Next rnd:** dc in pattern.
**Next rnd:** ch1, work in blo/flo patt as follows: 0[5:10:15]dc, *11dc, dc2tog; rep from * two more times, 4[9:24:34]dc, **dc2tog, 11dc, rep from ** to last 0[5:10:15]dc, dc in patt to end.
Work even in pattern (blo/flo) for 5 cm (2 in) or 28 cm (11 in) from armhole join.

## Hip Increases
**Next rnd:** ch1, work in blo/flo patt as follows: 0[5:10:15]dc, *11dc, 2dc in next st, rep from * two more times, 4dc, **2dc in next st, 11dc, rep from ** to last 0[5:10:15]dc, dc in patt to end.
**Next rnd:** Work even in patt.
**Next rnd:** ch1, work in flo/blo patt as follows: 20[25, 30,35]dc, 3dc in next st, 40dc, 3dc in next st, 20[25:30:35]dc.
**Next rnd:** Work even in patt.
**Next rnd:** ch1, work in flo/blo patt as follows: 22[27:32:37]dc, 3dc in next st, 40dc, 3dc in next st, 22[27:32:37]dc.

## Edging
**Rnd 1:** *miss 2 sts, work 5tr in 3rd st, miss 2 sts, sl st to next st, sl st in next 3 sts; rep from * around.
**Rnd 2:** sl st to first tr of rnd 1, ch4 (counts as 1tr, 1ch), *1tr in next tr, 1ch; rep from * around, sl st to 3rd ch of t-ch to join.
**Rnd 3:** sl st to 2nd tr of rnd 2, ch 4, 1tr in next tr, 1ch; rep from *, **tr2tog, 1ch, 1tr in next tr, 1ch; rep from ** to last 2 sts, tr2tog, 1ch, sl st to 3rd ch of t-ch to join. Fasten off.

Thread yarn with 180[200:220:240] pink beads.
**Rnd 4:** Rejoin yarn with a sl st to any 1ch-sp, place bead, ch1, place bead, ch1, *1tr in ch-sp, 1ch; rep from * around, sl st to chain above last bead in t-ch to join. Fasten off.

Thread yarn with 180[200:220:240] blue beads and rep rnd 4.

Thread yarn with 180[200:220:240] pink beads and rep rnd 4.

## Finishing
Weave in ends. Block gently.

# Hairpin Lace Top

Skill Level:
Advanced

The design
for the black
Pringle
openwork knit,
shown opposite
on the catwalk
for Spring/
Summer 2012,
translated
easily to
the hairpin
lace crochet
technique used
for this top,
right. Hairpin
lace is quick
to work up and
has gorgeous
effects,
making it
the ultimate
stitch for the
crocheter who
wants fast
results.

## Hairpin Lace Top
Claire Montgomerie

Hairpin lace is a crochet technique using a special hairpin tool, or loom, that was popular in the Victorian times. It provides a very open fabric, making garments perfect for layering over vests and T-shirts. This top is made in strips, which are crocheted together to form one seamless garment.

## YARN

4 x 50 g (2 oz) balls of Sublime Bamboo and Pearls
    DK, 70% bamboo sourced viscose, 30% pearl
    sourced viscose, 95 m (104 yds) in shade 210,
    Thai tea.

## NOTIONS

4 mm (size 8) crochet hook
Hairpin lace loom set at 10 cm (4 in) wide,
    or a 10 cm (4 in) hairpin loom

## MEASUREMENTS

Bust

| 81–86 | 91–96 | 102–106 | 111–116 cm |
|-------|-------|---------|------------|
| 32–34 | 36–38 | 40–42 | 44–45 in |

Length from Shoulder

| 44 | 48 | 54 | 60 cm |
|----|----|----|-------|
| 17 | 19 | 21 | 24 in |

## TENSION/GAUGE

Strips are worked 10 cm (4 in) wide and have
31 loops (both sides included) per 10 cm (4 in),
using a 4 mm (size 8) hook.

## PATTERN

With the loom set to 10 cm (4 in) width and using a 4 mm (size 8) hook, work 8[10:12:14] strips with 65[70:80:90] loops on each side and 2 strips of 140[150:170:190] loops on each side.

## Front

Join together 4[5:6:7] of the shorter strips in a cable join, picking up and drawing through 5 loops each time and not twisting the loops (the side facing you as you join the strips will be the RS).

## Back

Repeat as front with rem 4[5:6:7] strips.

## Sides

With RSF and working from the bottom up, join one long strip to the left-hand edge of the front 4[5:6:7] strip fabric using a sl st join, through one loop at a time, not twisting the loops.

Join the rem long strip to the right edge the same way.

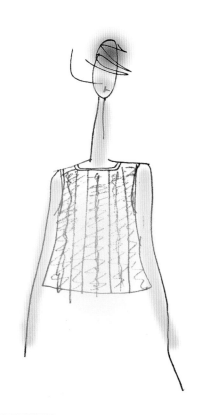

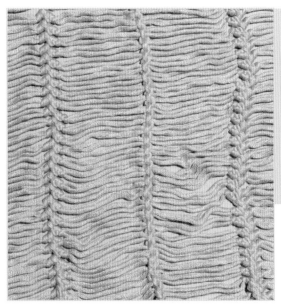

The long side strips are joined to the front and back using a slipstitch through one loop at a time. The schematic opposite shows how the pieces are stitched together to form the top.

Attach the rem 4[5:6:7] strip fabric in the same way to the other end of the long strips, as in the diagram below right, but when you reach the top of the short strip, complete inside neck/shoulder edge of either side as follows:

Do not fasten off yarn, 1ch, *insert hook into next loop above, yrh and pull through all lps on hook, rep from * in a sl st join until you reach top of back neck, sl st into top of back sl st join. Fasten off yarn.

Fold piece in half lengthways and, working from bottom, join either side seam with a sl st join through one loop at a time, without twisting the loops, for approx 24[28:32:36] cm, leaving armhole open, do not fasten off yarn, but continue to edge the armhole with a slipped stitch join all round as follows:

1ch, insert hook through next loop to left of join, without twisting, yrh, pull through all loops on hook, 1ch, *insert hook through next loop above, without twisting, yrh, pull through all loops on hook, 1ch; rep from * all round armhole, until you reach the top of the side seam join, sl st in first ch.
Fasten off.

### Neckband
Join yarn to neck at any point of edge, 1ch work dc evenly around entire neck, sl st in first dc to join round.

Weave in all ends and block lightly.

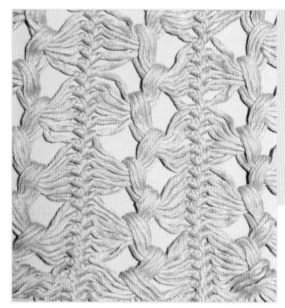

The front and back strips are joined together by a cable stitch, picking up sets of five loops at a time.

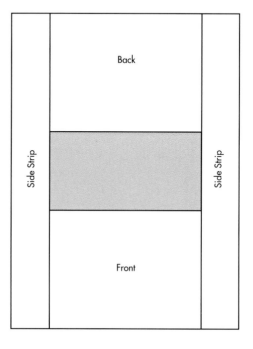

# Pineapple Halter Top

Skill Level:
Advanced

## Pineapple Halter Top

Victoria Stott

The Spring/Summer collections would not be complete without a bit of crochet and a halter top, and this stunning piece combines the two elements perfectly, with a very feminine swing "skirt" to the bottom of the garment that evokes traditional crocheted doilies and yet is far from old-fashioned. If you dare, this striking top could even be worn as a layering dress for a beach holiday.

### YARN
7[8:9:10] x 50 g (2 oz) balls of DMC Natura Just cotton, 100% combed cotton, 155 m (169 yds), in shade 16, tournesol

### NOTIONS
3 mm (size 11) crochet hook
Stitch markers

### MEASUREMENTS
Bust

| | | | |
|---|---|---|---|
| 81 | 86 | 91.5 | 96.5 cm |
| 32 | 34 | 36 | 38 in |

Length

| | | | |
|---|---|---|---|
| 92 | 95 | 95 | 95 cm |
| 36 | 37 | 37 | 37 in |

### TENSION/GAUGE
10 rows x 20 sts = 10 x10 cm (4 x 4 in) in main pattern (4tr, 1ch) using 3 mm (size 11) hook or size required to obtain correct tension.

### SPECIAL INSTRUCTIONS
**V Stitch (vst):** (2tr, 1ch, 2tr) in the same st or sp.
**Half V Stitch (½ vst):** (1tr, 1ch, 1tr) in the same st or sp.
**Shell (sh):** 2tr in the same st or sp.
**Bobble (bob):** 2tr together in the same st or sp.

The pineapple pattern in the yellow halter-neck dress by Ferragamo, above, was used to great effect in the tunic top project here. Traditionally used for doilies, the pineapple is a popular and versatile design with many variations – historically it was known as a symbol of hospitality, which may explain its commonplace use in table linens.

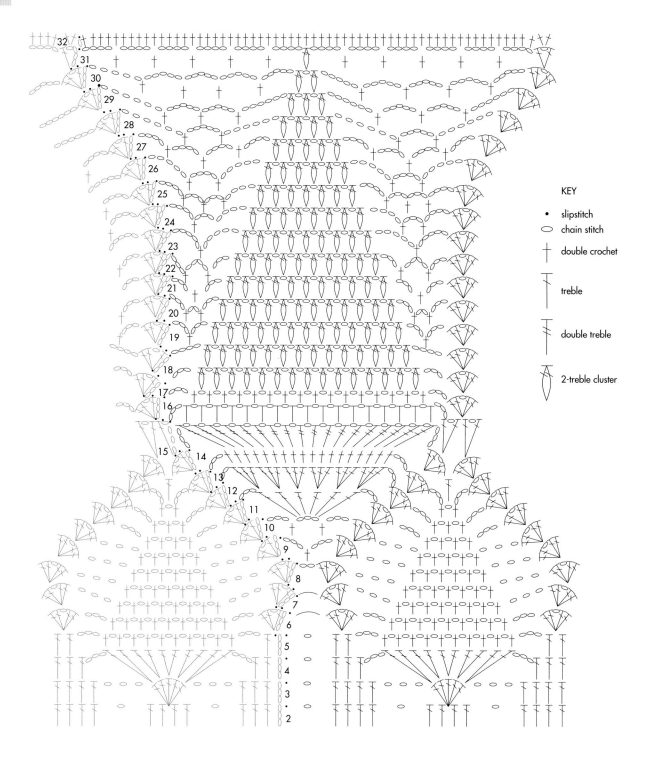

KEY

- slipstitch
- chain stitch
+ double crochet
| treble
|/ double treble
◊ 2-treble cluster

## PATTERN

### The Skirt (All Sizes)

**Foundation Round:** 193ch (use a larger hook so that the foundation chain is stretchy or, if you are able, start at rnd 1 as chainless foundation rnd), join to form ring using sl st, ensuring ch isn't twisted.

**Rnd 1:** ch 3 (counts as tr here and throughout), tr in next 3 ch, (1ch, miss 1 ch, tr in each of next 4 ch)x38, 1ch, miss last ch, join to 3rd ch of turning ch with sl st. *156 tr, 39 chsp.*

**Rnd 2:** 3ch, 3tr, (1ch, miss 1 chsp, 4tr)x38, 1ch, join to 3rd ch of turning ch with sl st.

**Rnd 3:** 3ch, 3tr, (*3ch, miss chsp, 5tr bet 2nd and 3rd tr of next 4-tr grp, 3ch, miss next chsp, 4tr, 1ch*, 4tr) x12; rep *to* once, join to 3rd ch of turning ch with sl st. *169 tr, 26 ch3sp.*

**Rnd 4:** 3ch, 2tr, [*3ch, miss (1tr, ch3sp), sh in each of next 5tr, 3ch, miss (ch3sp, 1tr), 3tr, 1ch, miss chsp*, 3tr]x12; rep *to* once, join to 3rd ch of turning ch with sl st. *208 tr.*

**Rnd 5:** 3ch, 1tr, [*3ch, miss (1tr, ch3sp), (1dc, 2ch) in each of next 9 tr, dc in next tr, 3ch, miss (ch3sp, 1tr), 2tr, 1ch*, 2tr]x12; rep *to* once, join to 3rd ch of turning ch with sl st. *52 tr, 130 dc, 117 ch2sp.*

**Rnd 6:** sl st bet turning ch and first tr, (3ch, 1tr, 1ch, sh) in same sp, [*3ch, (1dc, 2ch) in next 8 chsp, dc in next chsp, 3ch, vst bet next 2 tr*, miss chsp, vst bet next 2 tr]x12; rep *to* once, join to 3rd ch of first 3 ch of round with sl st.

**Rnd 7:** sl st in first tr and chsp in centre of vst, (3ch, 1tr, 1ch, sh) in same sp, [*3ch, miss ch3sp, (1dc, 2ch) in next 7 chsp, dc in next chsp, 3ch, vst in vst*, vst in next vst]x12; rep *to* once, join with sl st to top of first st of first vst.

**Rnd 8:** sl st in first tr and chsp in centre of vst, (3ch, 1tr, 1ch, sh) in same sp, [*3ch, miss ch3sp, (1dc, 2ch) in next 6 chsp, dc in next chsp, 3ch, vst in vst, 2ch*, vst in next vst]x12; rep *to* once, join with sl st to top of first st of first vst.

**Rnd 9:** sl st in first tr and chsp in centre of vst, (3ch, 1tr, 1ch, sh) in same sp, [*3ch, miss ch3sp, (1dc, 2ch) in next 5 chsp, dc in next chsp, 3ch, vst in vst, 3ch, 1dc in ch2sp, 3ch*, vst in next vst]x12; rep *to* once, join with sl st to top of first st of first vst.

**Rnd 10:** sl st in first tr and chsp in centre of vst, (3ch, 1tr, 1ch, sh) in same sp, [*3ch, miss ch3sp, (1dc, 2ch) in next 4 chsp, dc in next chsp, 3ch, vst in vst, (3ch, 1dc in ch3sp) twice, 3ch*, vst in next vst,]x12; rep *to* once, join with sl st to top of first st of first vst.

**Rnd 11:** sl st in first tr and chsp in centre of vst, (3ch, 1tr, 1ch, sh) in same sp, [*3ch, miss ch3sp, (1dc, 2ch) in next 3 chsp, dc in next chsp, 3ch, vst in vst, 3ch, miss ch3sp, 6tr in next ch3sp, miss ch3sp, 3ch*, vst in vst]x12; rep *to* once, join with sl st to top of first st of first vst.

**Rnd 12:** sl st in first tr and chsp in centre of vst, (3ch, 1tr, 1ch, sh) in same sp, [*3ch, miss ch3sp, (1dc, 2ch) in next 2 chsp, dc in next chsp, 3ch, vst in vst, 3ch, 3tr in each of next 6 tr, 3ch*, vst in vst]x12; rep *to* once, join with sl st to top of first st of first vst.

**Rnd 13:** sl st in first tr and chsp in centre of vst, (3ch, 1tr, 1ch, sh) in same sp, [*3ch, miss ch3sp, dc in next chsp, 2ch, dc in next chsp, 3ch, vst in vst, 3ch, dc in each of next 18 tr, 3ch*, vst in vst]x12; rep *to* once, join with sl st to top of first st of first vst.

**Rnd 14:** sl st in first tr and chsp in centre of vst, (3ch, 1tr, 1ch, sh) in same sp, [miss (ch3sp, dc), tr in ch2sp, miss (dc, ch3sp), vst in vst, 3ch, (1dtr, 1ch) in each of next 17 dc, 1dtr in next dc, 3ch*, vst in vst]x12; rep *to* once, join with sl st to top of first st of first vst.

**Rnd 15:** sl st in first tr and chsp in centre of vst, (4ch, 1tr) in same sp, [*3ch, miss first dtr, (1htr in next chsp, 1ch) 16 times, htr in next chsp, 3ch, ½vst in vst*, ½vst in next vst]x12; rep *to* once, join with sl st to 3rd ch of first 4ch.

**Rnd 16:** 3ch, (1tr, 1ch, 2tr) in sp between last and first ½vst of prev rnd, [*3ch, (1dc in next chsp, 1ch)x15, 1dc in next chsp, 3ch*, vst in space between next two ½vst]x12; rep *to* once, join with sl st to top of first ch3.

**Rnd 17:** sl st in first tr and chsp in centre of vst, (3ch, 1tr, 1ch, sh) in same sp, [*3ch, (bob in next chsp, 1ch)x14, bob in last chsp, 3ch*, vst in vst] x12; rep *to* once, join with sl st to top of first ch3.

**Rnd 18:** sl st in first tr and chsp in centre of vst, (3ch, 1tr, 1ch, sh) in same sp, [*4ch, (bob in next chsp, 1ch)x13, bob in last chsp, 4ch*, vst in vst] x12; rep *to* once, join with sl st to top of first ch3.

**Rnd 19:** sl st in first tr and chsp in centre of vst, (3ch, 1tr, 1ch, sh) in same sp, [*3ch, dc in ch4sp, 3ch, (bob in next chsp, 1ch)x12, bob in last chsp, 3ch, dc in ch4sp, 3ch*, vst in vst] x12; rep *to* once, join with sl st to top of first ch3.

**Rnd 20:** sl st in first tr and chsp in centre of vst, (3ch, 1tr, 1ch, sh) in same sp, [*3ch, dc in ch3sp, 2ch, dc in ch3sp, 3ch, (bob in next chsp, 1ch)x11, bob in last chsp, 3ch, dc in ch3sp, 2ch, dc in ch3sp, 3ch*, vst in vst] x12; rep *to* once, join with sl st to top of first ch3.

**Rnd 21:** sl st in first tr and chsp in centre of vst, (3ch, 1tr, 1ch, sh) in same sp, [*3ch, miss ch3sp, dc in ch2sp, miss c3sp, 3ch, (bob in next chsp, 1ch)x10, bob in last chsp, 3ch, miss ch3sp, dc in ch2sp, miss c3sp, 3ch*, vst in vst] x12; rep *to* once, join with sl st to top of first ch3.

**Rnd 22:** sl st in first tr and chsp in centre of vst, (3ch, 1tr, 1ch, sh) in same sp, [*3ch, dc in ch3sp, 4ch, dc in ch3sp, 3ch, (bob in next chsp, 1ch)x9, bob in last chsp, 3ch, dc in ch3sp, 4ch, dc in ch3sp, 3ch*, vst in vst] x12; rep *to* once, join with sl st to top of first ch3.

**Rnd 23:** sl st in first tr and chsp in centre of vst, (3ch, 1tr, 1ch, sh) in same sp, [*5ch, dc in ch4sp, 5ch, (bob in next chsp, 1ch)x8, bob in last chsp, 5ch, dc in ch4sp, 5ch*, vst in vst] x12; rep *to* once, join with sl st to top of first ch3.

**Rnd 24:** sl st in first tr and chsp in centre of vst, (3ch, 1tr, 1ch, sh) in same sp, [*4ch, dc in ch5sp, 3ch, dc in ch5sp, 4ch, (bob in next chsp, 1ch)x7, bob in last chsp, 4ch, dc in ch5sp, 3ch, dc in ch5sp, 4ch*, vst in vst]x12; rep *to* once, join with sl st to top of first ch3.

**Rnd 25:** sl st in first tr and chsp in centre of vst, (3ch, 1tr, 1ch, sh) in same sp, [*4ch, dc in ch4sp, 3ch, dc in ch3sp, 3ch, dc in ch4sp, 4ch, (bob in next chsp, 1ch)x6, bob in last chsp, 4ch, dc in ch4sp, 3ch, dc in ch3sp, 3ch, dc in ch4sp, 4ch *, vst in vst] x12; rep *to* once, join with sl st to top of first ch3.

**Rnd 26:** sl st in first tr and chsp in centre of vst, (3ch, 1tr, 1ch, sh) in same sp, [*5ch, miss ch4sp, dc in first ch3sp, 4ch, dc in next ch3sp, miss ch4sp, 5ch, (bob in next chsp, 1ch)x5, bob in last chsp, 5ch, miss ch4sp, dc in first ch3sp, 4ch, dc in next ch3sp, miss ch4sp, 5ch*, vst in vst] x12; rep *to* once, join with sl st to top of first ch3.

**Rnd 27:** sl st in first tr and chsp in centre of vst, (3ch, 1tr, 1ch, sh) in same sp, [*4ch, dc in ch5sp, 4ch, dc in ch4sp, 4ch, dc in 5chsp, 4ch, (bob in next chsp, 1ch)x4, bob in last chsp, 4ch, dc in ch5sp, 4ch, dc in ch4sp, 4ch, dc in 5chsp, 4ch*, vst in vst] x12; rep *to* once, join with sl st to top of first ch3.

**Rnd 28:** sl st in first tr and chsp in centre of vst, (3ch, 1tr, 1ch, sh) in same sp, [*6ch, dc in 2nd ch4sp, 5ch, dc in next ch4sp, 6ch, miss ch4sp, (bob in next chsp, 1ch)x3, bob in last chsp, 6ch, dc in 2nd ch4sp, 5ch, dc in next ch4sp, 6ch, miss ch4sp *, vst in vst]x12; rep *to* once, join with sl st to top of first ch3.

**Rnd 29:** sl st in first tr and chsp in centre of vst, (3ch, 1tr, 1ch, sh) in same sp, [*6ch, dc in ch6sp, 5ch, dc

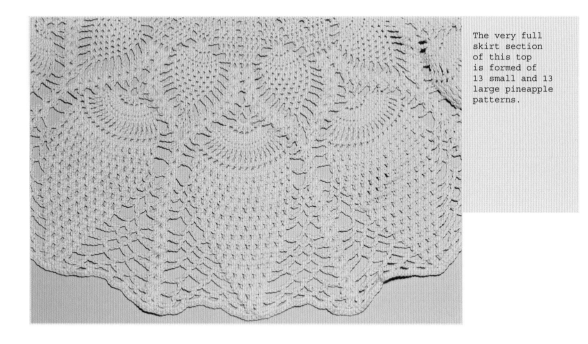

The very full
skirt section
of this top
is formed of
13 small and 13
large pineapple
patterns.

in ch5sp, 5ch, dc in ch6sp, 6ch, (bob in next chsp,
1ch)x2, bob in last chsp, 6ch, dc in ch6sp, 5ch, dc
in ch5sp, 5ch, dc in ch6sp, 6ch*, vst in vst] x12; rep
*to* once, join with sl st to top of first ch3.

**Rnd 30:** sl st in first tr and chsp in centre of vst,
(3ch, 1tr, 1ch, sh) in same sp, [*5ch, dc in ch6sp,
5ch, dc in ch5sp, 5ch, dc in ch5sp, 5ch, dc in
ch6sp, 5ch, bob in next ch1sp, 1ch, bob in last
ch1sp, 5ch, dc in ch6sp, 5ch, dc in ch5sp, 5ch,
dc in ch5sp, 5ch, dc in ch6sp, 5ch*, vst in vst]x12;
rep *to* once, join with sl st to top of first ch3.

**Rnd 31:** sl st in first tr and chsp in centre of vst,
(4ch, 1tr) in same sp, [*(4ch, dc in next ch5sp)x5,
4ch, bob in next ch1sp, (4ch, dc in next ch5sp)x5,
4ch*, (½vst in vst] x12; rep *to* once, join with sl st
to 3rd ch of ch4.

**Rnd 32:** sl st in first tr, 1ch, 2dc in chsp, [*(4dc in
ch4sp, 1dc in next dc)x5, 4dc in ch4sp, 1dc in bob,

(4dc in ch4sp, 1dc in next dc)x5, 4dc in ch4sp*, 2dc
in ch1sp]x12; rep *to* once, join with sl st to first ch.
Fasten off.

### The Bodice
Turn your work upside-down, find the base of a large
pineapple and with a finger, trace the chain spaces
down till you find the chain space column between two
v-stitches and continue to foundation chain. Mark this
chain space as the centre back of the garment.

With a sl st join in the opposite side of the foundation
chain in the first ch to the right of the marker.

### Sizes 8 & 10 Only
**Rnd 1:** 3ch, 2trtog, 1tr, 1ch, miss chsp, (1tr, 2trtog, 1tr,
1ch, miss chsp)x 3, (4tr, 1ch, miss chsp)x2, *1tr, 2trtog,
1tr, 1ch, miss chsp, (4tr, 1ch, miss chsp)x4; rep from *
4 more times, 1tr, 2trtog, 1tr, 1ch, miss chsp, (4tr, 1ch,
miss chsp)x2, (1tr, 2trtog, 1tr, 1ch, miss chsp)x4, sl st to
top of ch-3 to join. *181 sts*.

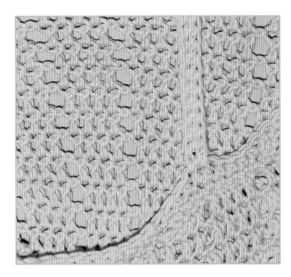

**Rnd 2:** 3ch, 2tr, 1tr, 1ch, miss chsp, (1tr, 2trtog, 1ch, miss chsp)x 3, (4tr, 1ch, miss chsp)x2, *1tr, 2trtog, 1ch, miss chsp, (4tr, 1ch, miss chsp)x4; rep from * 4 more times; 1tr, 2trtog, 1ch, miss chsp, (4tr, 1ch, miss chsp) x2, (1tr, 2trtog, 1ch, miss chsp)x4, sl st to top of ch-3 to join. *167 sts.*

**Rnd 3:** 3ch, tr in each tr and 1ch and miss over each chsp around, sl st to top of ch-3 to join.

**Rnd 4:** 3ch, 1tr, 1ch, miss chsp, (2tr, 1ch, miss chsp) x 3, (4tr, 1ch, miss chsp)x2, *2tr, 1ch, miss chsp, (4tr, 1ch, miss chsp)x4; rep from * 4 more times, 2tr, 1ch, miss chsp, (4tr, 1ch, miss chsp)x2, (2tr, 1ch, miss chsp) x4, sl st to top of ch-3 to join.

**Rnd 5:** 3ch, 1tr, miss chsp, 2tr, 1ch, miss chsp, 2tr, miss chsp, 2tr, 1ch, (4tr, 1ch, miss chsp)x2, *2trtog, 1ch, miss chsp, (4tr, 1ch, miss chsp)x4; rep from * 4 more times, 2trtog, 1ch, miss chsp, (4tr, 1ch, miss chsp)x2, (2tr, miss chsp, 2tr, 1ch)x2, sl st to top of ch-3 to join. *157 sts.*

**Rnd 6:** 3ch, 3tr, (1ch, miss chsp, 4tr)x3, *1ch, miss (chsp, 2trtog, chsp), (4tr, 1ch, miss chsp)x3, 4tr; rep

from * 4 more times; 1ch, miss (chsp, 2trtog, chsp), (4tr, 1ch, miss chsp)x4, sl st to top of ch-3 to join. *145 sts.*

## Size 10 Only
**Rnds 7–12:** 3ch, tr in each tr and 1ch and miss over each ch sp around, sl st to top of ch-3 to join.

## Size 8 Only
**Rnd 7:** 3ch, 1tr, 2trtog, 1ch, miss chsp, *(4tr, 1ch, miss chsp)x3**, (1tr, 2trtog, 1tr, 1ch, miss chsp)x2*, 4tr, 1ch, miss chsp, rep bet * and *, (4tr, 1ch, miss chsp) x2, rep bet * and *, 4tr, 1ch, miss chsp; rep bet * and *'; rep bet * and **, 1tr, 2trtog, 1tr, 1ch, miss chsp, sl st to top of ch-3 to join. *135 sts.*

**Rnd 8:** 3ch, 2trtog, 1ch, miss chsp, *(4tr, 1ch, miss chsp)x3**, (2trtog, 1tr, 1ch, miss chsp)x2*, 4tr, 1ch, miss chsp, rep bet * and *, (4tr, 1ch, miss chsp)x2, rep bet * and *, 4tr, 1ch, miss chsp; rep bet * and *';rep bet * and **, 1tr, 2trtog, 1ch, miss chsp, sl st to top of ch-3 to join. *125 sts.*

**Rnd 9:** 3ch, 1tr, 1ch, miss chsp, *(4tr, 1ch, miss chsp) x3**, (2tr, 1ch, miss chsp)x2*, 4tr, 1ch, miss chsp, rep bet * and *, (4tr, 1ch, miss chsp)x2, rep bet * and *, 4tr, 1ch, miss chsp; rep bet * and *';rep bet * and **, 2tr, 1ch, miss chsp, sl st to top of ch-3 to join.

**Rnd 10:** 3ch, 1tr, 1ch, miss chsp, *(4tr, 1ch, miss chsp)x3**, 2tr, miss chsp, 2tr, 1ch, miss chsp*, 4tr, 1ch, miss chsp, rep bet * and *, (4tr, 1ch, miss chsp) x2, rep bet * and *, 4tr, 1ch, miss chsp; rep bet * and *';rep bet * and **, 2tr, miss chsp, sl st to top of ch-3 to join. *120 sts.*

**Rnds 11–12:** 3ch, tr in each tr and 1ch and miss over each chsp around, sl st to top of ch-3 to join.

## Size 12 Only
**Rnd 1:** 3ch, 2trtog, 1tr, 1ch, miss chsp, (1tr, 2trtog, 1tr, 1ch, miss chsp)x2, *(4tr, 1ch, miss chsp)x8, (1tr, 2trtog, 1tr, 1ch, miss chsp)x2*, (4tr, 1ch, miss chsp)x5; rep bet * and * twice, 1tr, 2trtog, 1tr, 1ch, miss chsp, sl st to top of ch-3 to join. *185 sts.*

**Rnd 2:** 3ch, 2trtog, 1ch, miss chsp, (2trtog, 1tr, 1ch, miss chsp)x2, *(4tr, 1ch, miss chsp)x8, (2trtog, 1tr, 1ch, miss chsp)x2*, (4tr, 1ch, miss chsp)x5; rep bet * and * twice, 2trtog, 1tr, 1ch, miss chsp, sl st to top of ch-3 to join. *175 sts.*

**Rnd 3:** 3ch, 1tr, 1ch, miss chsp, (2tr, 1ch, miss chsp)x2, *(4tr, 1ch, miss chsp)x8, (2tr, 1ch, miss chsp)x2*, (4tr, 1ch, miss chsp)x5; rep bet * and * twice, 2tr, 1ch, miss chsp, sl st to top of ch-3 to join.

**Rnd 4:** 3ch, 1tr, 1ch, miss chsp, *2tr, miss chsp, 2tr, 1ch, miss chsp, (4tr, 1ch, miss chsp)x8*, rep bet * and *, (4tr, 1ch, miss chsp)x5; rep bet *and*, 2tr, miss chsp, 2tr, 1ch, miss chsp, 2tr, miss chsp, sl st to top of ch-3 to join. *170 sts.*

**Rnds 5–12:** 3ch, tr in each tr and 1ch and miss over each chsp around, sl st to top of ch-3 to join.

## Size 14 Only
**Rnd 1:** 3ch, 2trtog, 1tr, 1ch, miss chsp, (4tr, 1ch, miss chsp) rep across to last 4 tr, 1tr, 2trtog, 1tr, 1ch, miss chsp, sl st to top of ch-3 to join. *193 sts.*

**Rnd 2:** 3ch, 2trtog, 1ch, miss chsp, (4tr, 1ch, miss chsp) rep across to last 3 tr, 2trtog, 1tr, 1ch, miss chsp, sl st to top of ch-3 to join. *191 sts.*

**Rnd 3:** 3ch, 1tr, 1ch, miss chsp, (4tr, 1ch, miss chsp) rep across to last 2 tr, 2tr, miss chsp, sl st to top of ch-3 to join. *190 sts.*

**Rnds 4–12:** 3ch, tr in each tr and 1ch and miss over each chsp around, sl st to top of ch-3 to join.

## First Side of Halter
**Row 1:** Sl st across 11 [11:16:16] sts (last sl st should be in first tr of group of 4 tr), 3ch, place marker in 3rd ch, 3tr, (1ch, miss chsp, 4tr)x 20[24:27:31], turn, leaving rem sts unworked. *84[96:108:124] tr.*

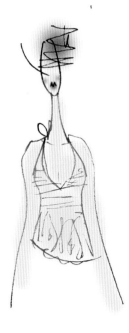

## Size 8 Only
**Row 2:** sl st across 6 sts (last one should be in first tr of group of 4tr), **3ch, 3tr, (1ch, miss chsp, 4tr)x4, 1ch, 3tr, 2tr in next tr, 1ch, miss chsp, 2tr in next tr, 3tr, 1ch, 4tr, 1ch, 2tr, turn leaving rem sts unworked. *36 tr.*

**Row 3:** 3ch, 1tr, miss (chsp, 1tr), 3tr, 1ch, 4tr, 1ch, 2tr in next tr, miss chsp, 2tr in next tr, 1ch, 4tr, (1ch, miss chsp, 4tr)x4, miss chsp, 2trtog. *33 tr and 1 dec.*

## Sizes 10, 12, 14 Only
**Row 2:** sl st across [11:21:11] sts (last one should be in first tr of group of 4tr), 3ch, 3tr, (1ch, miss chsp, 4tr)x[5:5:8], 1ch, 3tr, (2tr in next tr, 2tr)x2, 1tr, 1ch, 4tr, 1ch, 2tr, turn leaving rem sts unworked. *46:46:58 tr.*

**Row 3:** 3ch, 1tr, miss (chsp, 1tr), 3tr, 1ch, (4tr, 1ch, 2tr in next tr, miss chsp, 2tr in next tr, 1ch)x2, 4tr, (1ch, miss chsp, 4tr)x[5:5:8], miss chsp, 2trtog, turn. *43:43:55 tr and 1 dec.*

## All Sizes
**Row 4:** 3ch, miss 1tr, 2trtog, 1tr, *1ch, miss chsp, 4tr; rep across to last 4 tr, 2tr, 2trtog, turn. *28 [38:38:50] tr and 2 dec.*

**Row 5:** 3ch, 2trtog, (1ch, miss chsp, 4tr)x 6[9:9:9], 1ch, miss chsp, 2trtog, [size 14 only, (2trtog, 1ch, miss chsp, 2trtog) twice]. Turn.

## Sizes 8, 10, 12 Only
**Row 6:** 3ch, miss (chsp, 1tr), 2trtog, 1tr, (1ch, miss chsp, 2trtog, 2trtog)x 0[2:2], (1ch, miss chsp, 4tr) x5[6:6], miss chsp, 1tr. Turn.

## Size 14 Only
**Row 6:** 3ch, 2tr, miss chsp, 2tr, (1ch, miss chsp, 2trtog, 2trtog)x2, (1ch, miss chsp, 4tr)x7, miss chsp, 1tr. Turn.

## All Sizes
**Row 7:** 3ch, miss (chsp, 1tr), 3tr, (1ch, miss chsp, 4 tr) x4[5:5:6], (1ch, 2tr, miss chsp, 2tr, 1ch, miss chsp) x0[1:1:1], [size 14 only 4tr, turn], miss chsp, 2trtog. Turn.

**Row 8:** 3ch, miss chsp, 2trtog, 2trtog, (1ch, miss chsp, 2trtog, 2trtog)x0[1:1:2], (1ch, miss chsp, 4tr)x3 [4:4:5], 1ch, miss chsp, 3tr. Turn.

### Size 8 Only
**Row 9:** 3ch, 2trtog, 1ch, 2trtog, 2trtog, (1ch, miss chsp, 4tr)x2, 1ch, miss chsp, 2trtog.

**Row 10:** 4ch, 2trtog, 2trtog, 1ch, miss chsp, 4tr, 1ch, miss chsp, 2trtog, 1tr, turn.

**Row 11:** Skip to Row 13.

### Sizes 10 & 12 Only
**Row 9:** 3ch, 2trtog, 1ch miss chsp, 4tr, 1ch, miss chsp, 2trtog, 2trtog, (1ch, miss chsp, 4tr)x2, (1ch, miss chsp, 2tr)x2. Turn.

### Size 14 Only
**Row 9:** 3ch, 2trtog, (1ch, miss chsp, 2trtog, 2trtog)x3, (1ch, miss chsp, 4tr)x2, (1ch, miss chsp, 2tr)x2. Turn.

### Sizes 10, 12, 14 Only
**Row 10:** (Missing all chsps, and working all tr into tr) 3ch, (2trtog, 2trtog, 1ch)x2, 1ch, 4tr, 1ch, 2tr, 1ch, 4tr, 1ch, 1tr. Turn.

**Row 11:** (Missing all chsps, and working all tr into tr) 3ch, (2trtog)x3, 1ch, 4tr, 1ch, 2tr, 1ch, 2tr. Turn.

**Row 12:** 3ch, 1tr, miss chsp, 2tr, 1ch, miss chsp, 4tr, 1ch, miss chsp, 1tr, 1ch, 2tr. Turn.

### All Sizes
**Row 13:** 3ch, miss (1tr, chsp), 1tr, 1ch, miss chsp, 4t, 1ch, miss chsp, 2trtog, 1tr. Fasten off.

### Second Side of Halter
With RS facing, from marked stitch on row 1 of First Side of Halter, count 9[9:13:13] tr towards First Side and join with sl st in first tr of this 4tr group.

Work from ** in row 2 of First Side across. Work rows 3–13 as in First Side of Halter.

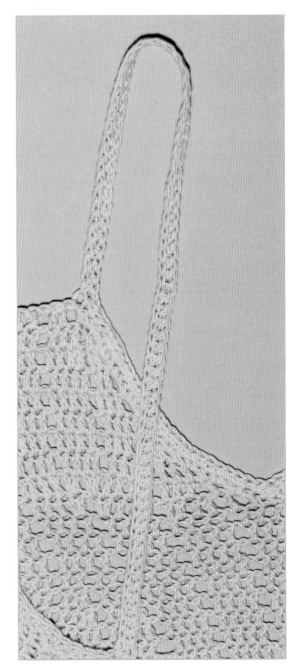

## Halter Strap (All Sizes)

**Row 1:** Starting in centre back stitch, join yarn with sl st and 1ch, dc around evenly working 1dc into stitch tops and 3dc into sides of tr sts. Do not add extra sts into corners, sl st to first ch to join.

**Row 2:** 2ch, 1htr in each dc along the back and underarm curve up to top of halter side, sl st into first st of halter top, 80ch, making sure the ch is not twisted, join with sl st to dc at top outer edge of second halter side, 1htr in each dc around second underarm curve and along back, sl st to join in ch2.

**Row 3:** 1ch, 1dc in each st around to halter strap, 1tr in each ch of strap, 1dc in each st returning to centre back, sl st to join in first ch.
Fasten off.

## Shoulder Straps (All Sizes)

**Row 1:** Count 15 and 18 sts to either side of centre back and place stitch markers, with RS facing, join with sl st to top inside corner of left halter side at the neckline, 70ch, making sure ch is not twisted, join with sl st to back at marked st, 3ch, sl st in 15th st from centre back on same side, 1ch, turn, 1tr in each ch of strap, 1htr in each stitch down v-neck opening, 3htr in centre st between bust pieces, 1htr in each st up v-neck opening, 70ch, making sure ch is not twisted, join with sl st to 15th st from centre back, 3ch, sl st in 18th st on same side, 1ch, turn, 1tr in each ch along the strap, join with sl st to top corner of right halter side at neckline.
Fasten off.

## Finishing
Weave in all ends.

# Cornflower Fringe Top

Skill Level:
Intermediate

## Cornflower Fringe Top

Claire Montgomerie

This very simple top mixes a basic crocheted fabric with some pretty hairpin mesh and fringing for great effect, resulting in a very pretty textural summer shell, perfect for hairpin beginners. The hairpin strips can be left free on one edge and used for a fringe, creating an embellishment that has been a notable trend for a few seasons.

### YARN
8[8:9:10] x 50g (2 oz) balls of Bessie May Bee, 100% cotton, 100 m (109 yds) in shade 8390, bell

### NOTIONS
4 mm (size 8) crochet hook
Hairpin loom set to 10 cm (4 in) wide or 10 cm (4 in) hairpin loom
Tapestry needle

### MEASUREMENTS
Bust

| | | | |
|---|---|---|---|
| 82 | 86 | 91 | 96.5 cm |
| 32 | 34 | 36 | 38 in |

Actual Size

| | | | |
|---|---|---|---|
| 85 | 89 | 94 | 100 cm |
| 33½ | 35 | 37¾ | 39¼ in |

Length (incl fringe)

| | | | |
|---|---|---|---|
| 66 | 66 | 67 | 67 cm |
| 26 | 26 | 26¼ | 26¼ in |

### TENSION/GAUGE
17htr and 13 rows over 10 cm (4 in) using 4 mm (size 6) crochet hook or size required to obtain correct tension.

An openwork crochet top with deep fringing from Gucci, above, gives a slightly ethnic feel in this neutral taupe shade. The cornflower blue version, opposite, provides more modest coverage, combining hairpin detailing at the yoke and fringe with chainstitching for the body of the piece.

## PATTERN
### Front Yoke

Using 4 mm (size 6) hook and hairpin loom set to 10 cm (4 in) wide, work a strip with 44[44:52:52] loops on each side.

Edge strip at neck edge as folls:
Insert hook through first 2 lps of one side of strip from front to back, twist lps 3 times. Attach yarn through these 2 lps and work 1ch to secure. 4ch, insert hook through next 2 lps along from front to back, twist lps 3 times, 1ch to secure, 4ch, *insert hook through each of next 4 lps along from front to back, 1ch to secure, 4ch, (insert hook through each of next 2 lps along from front to back, twist loops 3 times, 1ch to secure, 4ch) twice; rep from * to end of strip, omitting last 4ch. Turn.

3ch, work 75[77:81:85]htr evenly along edge of strip. Turn and work one row straight in htr on these 75[77:81:85] sts.

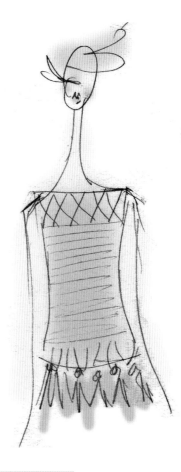

The top is formed of simple rectangular front and back pieces, with the hairpin yoke stitched to the shorter front and the fringe attached at the hem, as shown in the schematic opposite.

## Front Body

Rep edging for opposite side of strip, but continue on these 75[77:81:85] sts until front measures 58[58:59:59] cm (23[23:23¼:23¼] in) in total including hairpin yoke, or desired length.

## Back Body

Using 4 mm (size 8) hook, ch77[79:83:87].
**Row 1:** Work 1 htr into 3rd ch from hook, then work 1 htr into each ch to end of row. Turn. 75[77:81:85] sts.
**Row 2:** ch 2, 1 htr into each st to end of row.
Rep row 2 until back measures same as front (including hairpin section). Fasten off yarn.

## Finishing

Weave in all ends and block lightly to shape.
Seam top edges of pieces along yoke for 10[10:11:12] cm (4[4:4¼:4¾] in) in from each side to create shoulder seams, leaving centre open for neck.

Sew up side seams, leaving top 21[21:22:22] cm (8¼[8¼:8½:8½] in) open for armholes.

## Armholes

Attach yarn to any point around armhole and work a row of dc evenly around armhole opening, join with sl st into round and then work one further round on these sts. Fasten off yarn. Rep for rem armhole.

## Fringed Hem

Using 4 mm (size 8) hook and hairpin loom set to 10 cm (4 in) wide, work a strip with 88[88:104:104] loops on each side.

Edge and join one side of strip to body as follows, leaving rem side free to create fringe.

Insert hook through first 2 lps of one side of strip from front to back, twist lps 3 times. Attach yarn through these 2 lps and work 1 ch to secure, sl st to hem of top at one side seam. Work edging as on yoke strip, joining at regular intervals to the hem of top using a sl st join. It is best to place a sl st joining stitch halfway through each 4ch you make along the edge.

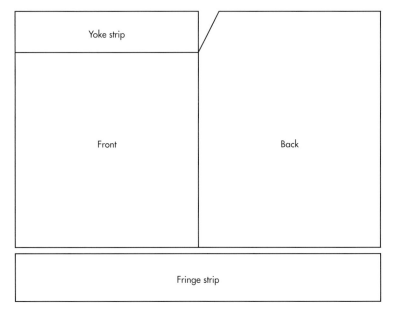

# Colour Block Jumper

Skill Level:
Advanced

Colour-block
knitwear
from the
Milan-based
label Etro,
opposite,
provided
inspiration
for this
intarsia
crochet jumper
in blocks of
pink, blue and
grey. The silk
content of the
yarn makes the
jumper lovely
to wear next to
the skin.

## Colour Block Jumper
Catherine Wilson

Geometric colour blocking has been a familiar trend for many seasons now. This top uses simple intarsia techniques mixed with bold stripes to create a striking geometric pattern, which would also look stunning in monochrome. The back is plain, but could easily be striped to fit in with the colour-block theme.

## YARN

4[4:5:5] x 100 g (4 oz) skeins of Fyberspates
Scrumptious 4-ply sport, 55% wool, 45% silk,
365 m (399 yds) in oyster (MC)
1 x 100 g (4 oz) skein each of Fyberspates
Scrumptious 4-ply sport, 55% wool, 45% silk, 365 m
(399 yds) in baby pink (yarn A), midnight (yarn B),
slate (yarn C), teal (yarn D)

## NOTIONS

3 mm (size 10) crochet hook
2.5 mm (size 12) crochet hook
Tapestry needle

## MEASUREMENTS

Bust

| 81 | 86 | 91 | 96 cm |
|----|----|----|-------|
| 32 | 34 | 36 | 38 in |

Actual Size

| 83 | 88 | 93 | 98 cm |
|----|----|----|-------|
| 32½ | 34½ | 36½ | 38½ in |

## TENSION/GAUGE

21 sts wide and 10 rows down over 10 cm
(4 in), unblocked.
20 sts wide and 9.5 rows down over 10 cm
(4 in), blocked.

## SPECIAL INSTRUCTIONS

Garment worked entirely in treble stitch unless
otherwise stated. Colour blocking using Intarsia
(separate balls of yarn used, as colours not in use
cannot be carried across the back of the work).

For Front piece, instructions for shaping are given.

The chart provides the details of stitches and rows
worked in different colours.

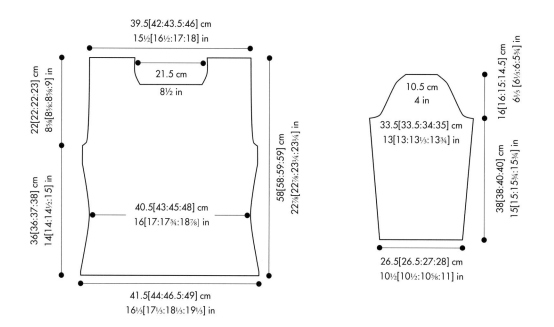

## PATTERN
### Back
Using 3 mm (size 11) hook and MC, commence at lower edge and use MC throughout.

**Foundation row:** 94[99:104:109] ch. Work 1tr into 4th ch from hk, 1tr into each tr to end. *91[96:101:106]tr.*

**Row 1:** 3ch (counts as 1tr) 1tr in each tr to end. *91[96:101:106]tr.*
**Row 2 (dec row):** 3ch, 2trtog, work 1tr in each st to the last 3 sts, 2trtog, tr in last st. *89[94:99:104]tr.*
**Row 3:** 3ch, tr into each st to end.
**Row 4:** Rep row 2. *87[92:97:102]tr.*
**Rows 5–7:** Rep row 3.
**Row 8:** Rep row 2. *85[90:95:100]tr.*
**Rows 9–11:** Rep row 3.
**Row 12:** Rep row 2. *83[88:93:98]tr.*
**Rows 13–15:** Rep row 3.
**Row 16:** Rep row 2. *81[86:91:96]tr.*
**Row 17–22:** Rep row 3.

**Row 23 (inc row):** 3ch, 2tr in next st, tr across to last 2 sts, 2tr in next st, tr in the last st. *83[88:93:98]tr.*
**Row 24–27:** Rep row 3.
**Row 28:** Rep row 23. *85[90:95:100]tr.*
**Row 29:** Rep row 23. *87[92:97:102]tr.*
**Row 30:** Rep row 23. *89[94:99:104]tr.*
**Row 31–34[34:35:36]:** Rep row 3.

### Shape Armhole
**Row 35[35:36:37]:** 1ch, sl st over next 4[4:5:5] sts, 3ch, 2trtog, tr in each st to last 6[6:7:7] tr. 2trtog, 1tr in next tr, turn leaving rem sts unworking.
**Row 36[36:37:38:]:** Rep row 2.
**Row 37[37:38:39]– 55[55:56:56]:** Rep row 3.

### Shape Right Shoulder
**Next row (WS[WS:RS:RS]):** 1ch, sl st into next 5[6:7:8] tr, 1dc into next 5[6:7:8] tr, tr into next 7[8:7:8] tr. Turn.
**Next row:** 3ch, tr into next 6[7:6:7] tr, 1dc into next 5[5:6:7] dc, sl st into each of next 5[7:8:9] sts. Break yarn. Fasten off.

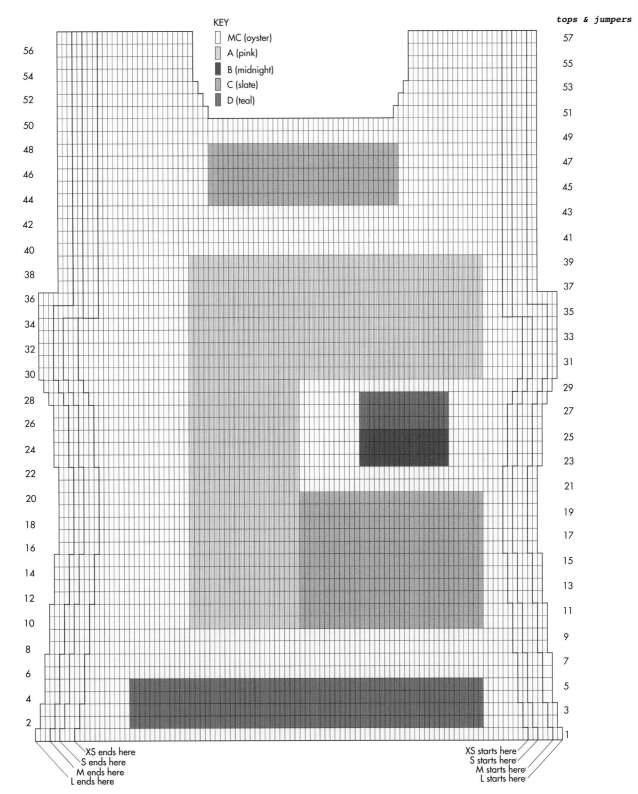

KEY

MC (oyster)
A (pink)
B (midnight)
C (slate)
D (teal)

XS ends here
S ends here
M ends here
L ends here

XS starts here
S starts here
M starts here
L starts here

### Shape Left Shoulder

**Next row:** With WS[WS:RS:RS] facing, with sl st join yarn 17[20:21:24] sts towards centre from left edge. 3ch tr in next 6[7:6:7] tr, dc in next 5[6:7:8] tr, sl st to end. Turn.

**Next row:** 1ch, sl st in next 5[7:8:9] sts, dc in next 5[5:6:7] dc, tr to end. Break yarn. Fasten off.

### Front

Work as for the Back up to row 51; however, follow chart for colourwork. To change a colour, work last tr of current colour until 2 loops remain on hook, yarn round hook with new colour, and draw through 2 loops. Work next stitch in new colour.

### Shape Front Neck
### Right Side

**Row 51(WS):** 3ch, 18[20:23:25] tr, (2trtog) twice, tr in next tr, leaving rem sts unworked. Turn. *22[24:27:29] sts.*

**Row 52:** 3ch, 2trtog, tr across. Turn. *21[23:26:28] sts.*

**Row 53:** 3ch, tr to last 3 sts, 2trtog, 1tr. Turn. *20[22:25:27] sts.*

**Row 54:** Rep row 52. *19[21:24:26] sts.*

**Rows 55–57:** Work straight without shaping. Break off yarn. Fasten off.

### Left Side

**Row 51(WS):** With sl st join yarn 24[26:29:31] sts towards centre from left edge. 3ch, (2trtog) twice, tr across. Turn. *22[24:27:29] sts.*

**Row 52:** 3ch, tr to last 3 sts, 2trtog, 1tr. Turn. *21[23:26:28] sts.*

**Row 53:** 3ch, 2trtog, tr across. Turn. *20[22:25:27] sts.*

**Row 54:** Rep row 52. *19[21:24:26] sts.*

**Rows 55–57:** Work straight without shaping. Break off yarn. Fasten off.

### Right Sleeve

**Foundation row:** Using 3 mm (size 10) hook and MC ch 56[56:57:59], work 1 tr into 4th ch from hk, 1tr into each ch to end. *53[53:54:56]tr.*

**Row 1:** 3ch, work 1tr into each tr across.

**Rows 2–4:** Rep row 1.

**Row 5:** 3ch, 2tr in next tr, tr across to last 2 sts, 2tr in next st, 1tr. Turn. *55[55:56:58]tr.*

**Rows 6–10:** Rep row 1.

**Row 11:** Rep row 5. *57[57:58:60]tr.*

**Rows 12–15:** Rep row 1.

**Row 16:** Rep row 5. *59[59:60:62]tr.*

**Rows 17–18:** Rep row 1, changing colour to A on last tr.

**Rows 19–22:** Rep row 1 continuing in A.

**Row 23:** Rep row 5 continuing in A. *61[61:62:64]tr.*

**Row 24:** Rep row 1 in A, changing to C at end of row.

**Rows 25–27:** Rep row 1 in C, changing colour to MC at end of row.

**Row 28:** Rep row 1 in MC (sleeve now continues to the end in MC).

**Row 29:** Rep row 5. *63[63:64:66]tr.*

**Rows 30–32:** Rep row 1.

**Row 33:** Rep row 5. *65[65:66:68]tr.*

**Row 34:** Rep row 1.

**Row 35:** Rep row 5. *67[67:68:70]tr.*

**Rows 36[36:36–38:36–38]:** Rep row 1, ending on a RS row.

### Sleeve Head
**Smaller Two Sizes:** Skip to row 39.

**Row 39:** 1ch, sl st in next 7[7:7:8]tr, 3ch work 1tr into each tr across, leaving the last 6[6:6:7]tr unworked. Turn. *55[55:56:56]tr.*
**Row 40:** 3ch, 2trtog, 1tr into each tr to the last 3tr, 2trtog, 1tr. *53[53:54:54]tr.*
**Row 41:** Rep row 40. *51[51:52:52]tr.*
**Row 42:** 3ch, (2trtog) twice, work to last 5 sts, (2trtog) twice, 1tr. *47[47:48:48]tr.*
**Row 43:** Rep row 40. *45[45:46:46]tr.*
**Row 44:** Rep row 42. *41[41:42:42]tr.*
**Rows 45–48:** Rep row 40. *33[33:34:34] tr after row 46.*
**Row 49:** Rep row 42. *29[29:30:30]tr.*
**Row 50:** Rep row 42. *25[25:26:26]tr.*
**Row 51:** Rep row 42. *21[21:22:22]tr.*

**Smaller Two Sizes:** Fasten off.

**Larger Two Sizes:**
**Row 52:** Rep row 40. *[21:21]tr.*

### Left Sleeve
Work as Right Sleeve, using the following colour stripe sequence instead:
**Row 11:** Change colour to D at the end of this row.
**Rows 12–16:** In D at the end of this row change colour to B.
**Rows 17–19:** In B change to MC at the end of the row. Continue in MC to the end of the sleeve.
Break off yarn. Fasten off.

### Making Up
Weave in ends, block lightly.
Using backstitch to make up, join shoulder seams, pin and sew in sleeves, join side and sleeve seams.

### Edging
Using 2.5 mm (size 12) hook and MC work 2 rows of dc evenly around hem, sleeves and neckline. Weave in ends.

# Chunky Cabled Cardigan

Skill Level:
Advanced

This chunky
dip-dye-effect
cardigan was
inspired by
the Missoni
catwalk
version
opposite,
worn over a
maxidress
to create a
long-line
silhouette.
With its
chunky cable
stitching and
long length,
it makes a
warm and cosy
cardigan-coat.

## Chunky Cabled Cardigan

Lesley Arnold Hopkins

Aran fabric is generally considered to be only achievable in knitting, but this textured cardigan uses all-over cables to create a chunky Aran-like quality. Wear the cardigan loose as a warm substitute to a coat or nipped in at the waist, buckled with an on-trend skinny belt to add shape to the bulky form.

## YARN
13[14:15:17] x 50 g (2 oz) balls of Drops Eskimo,
    100% wool, 50 m (55 yds) in shade 36, light
13[15:17:20] x 50 g (2 oz) balls of Drops Eskimo,
    100% wool, 50 m (55 yds) in shade 54, dark

## NOTIONS
8 mm (size 0) crochet hook

## MEASUREMENTS
Bust

| 72 | 82 | 93 | 103 cm |
|----|----|----|--------|
| 28 | 32 | 36 | 40 in  |

Actual Size

| 85 | 95  | 105 | 116 cm |
|----|-----|-----|--------|
| 33 | 37  | 41  | 45 in  |

## TENSION/GAUGE
10 sts x 5 rows to measure 10 x 10 cm (4 x 4 in) over
pattern, using size 8 mm (size 0) hook, or size required
to obtain tension.

## SPECIAL INSTRUCTIONS
**RdtrF** = raised double treble around the front of stitch.
**RdtrB** = raised double treble around the back of stitch.
**dtr2tog** = Work 2 sts tog, keeping pattern correct.

**Cable 6 Right, Front (C6RF):** Miss next 3 sts, work
1RdtrF around each of the next 3 sts. Going behind the
sts just worked, work 1dtr into each of the 3 sts missed.
**Cable 6 Left, Front (C6LF):** Miss the next 3 sts, work
1dtr into each of the next 3 sts. Going in front of
the sts just worked, work 1Rdtr F around each of the
3 sts missed.
**Cable 6 Left, Back (C6LB):** Miss the next 3 sts, work
1dtr into each of the next 3 sts. Going behind the sts
just worked, work 1 RdtrB around each of the 3 sts
missed.
**Cable 6 Right, Back (C6RB):** Miss the next 3 sts,
work 1dtr into each of the next 3 sts. Going in front
of the sts just worked, work 1 RdtrB around each of
the 3 sts missed.

## PATTERN
### Back
Using the lighter yarn, make 41[47:53:65] ch.

**Foundation row (WS):** Starting in the 3rd chain from the hook, work 1dc into each chain. *40[46,52,64] sts.*

**Row 1:** 3ch (for first tr), work 1tr into the next st, (C6RF, C6LF); repeat to last 2[8:2:2] sts, work C6RF 0[1:0:0] times, work 1tr into each of the last 2 sts.

**Row 2:** 3ch (for first tr), work 1tr into the next st. Work 1 RdtrB into each stitch to the last 2 sts. Work 1tr into each of the last 2 sts.

**Row 3:** 3ch (for first tr), work 1 tr into the next st. Work 1 RdtrF into each stitch to the last 2 sts. Work 1tr into each of the last 2 sts.

**Row 4:** As row 2.

**Row 5:** As row 3.

**Row 6:** 3ch (for first tr), work 1tr into the next st, work C6LB 0[1:0:0] times, (C6RB, C6LB); repeat to last 2 sts, work 1tr into each of the last 2 sts.

**Row 7:** As row 3.

**Row 8:** As row 2.

**Row 9:** As row 3.

**Row 10:** As row 2.

These 10 rows form the pattern.

Work a further 4 rows (bringing the total to 14) in the lighter colour, then change to the darker colour and work 9 rows in pattern.

### Shape Armhole
Keeping pattern correct:

**Row 26:** Work a sl st into each of the next 3[4:5:5] sts, then work 3ch (for the first tr). Work in patt until 2[3:4:4] sts from the end of the row. Turn.

**Row 27:** 3ch (for first tr), dtr2tog, work to last 3 sts, dtr2tog, work 1tr into the last st. Turn.

Repeat row 27 3[3:1:2] more times. *30[34:40:50] sts.* Work straight until number of rows completed in armhole is 8[10:12:14]. Fasten off yarn.

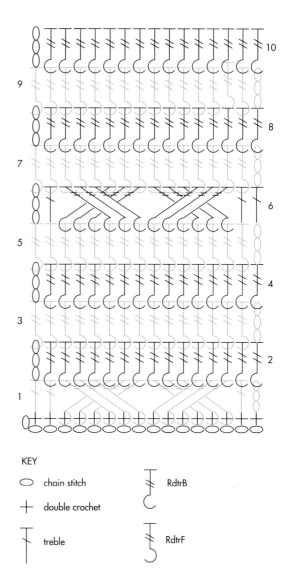

**KEY**

| | | |
|---|---|---|
| ⬭ chain stitch | | ⌁ RdtrB |
| + double crochet | | |
| ⌁ treble | | ⌁ RdtrF |

## Left Front

Using the lighter yarn, make 21[27:29:33] ch.
**Foundation row (WS):** Starting in the 3rd chain from the hook, work 1dc into each chain. *20[26:28:32] sts.*
**Row 1:** 3ch (for first tr), work 1tr into the next 0[0:1:0] sts, (C6RF, C6LF); repeat to last 7[1:2:7] sts, work C6RF 1[0:0:1] times, work 1tr into each st to end.
**Row 2:** 3ch (for first tr), work 1tr into the next st. Work 1 RdtrB into each stitch to the last 2 sts. Work 1tr into each of the last 2 sts.
**Row 3:** 3ch (for first tr), work 1tr into the next st. Work 1 RdtrF into each stitch to the last 2 sts. Work 1tr into each of the last 2 sts.
**Row 4:** As row 2.
**Row 5:** As row 3.
**Row 6:** 3ch (for first tr), work 1tr into the next 0[0:1:0] sts, work C6LB1[0:0:1] times, (C6RB, C6LB); repeat to last 1[1:2:1] sts, work 1tr into each st to end.
**Row 7:** As row 3.
**Row 8:** As row 2.
**Row 9:** As row 3.
**Row 10:** As row 2.
These 10 rows form the pattern.

Work a further 4 rows (bringing the total to 14) in the lighter colour, then change to the darker colour and work 9 rows in pattern.

## Shape Armhole

Keeping pattern correct.
**Row 26:** Work a sl st into each of the next 3[4:5:5] sts, then work 3ch (for the first tr). Work in patt until 3 sts from the end of the row, dtr2tog, 1 tr into the last st.
**Row 27:** 3ch (for first tr), dtr2tog, work to last 3 sts, dtr2tog, work 1tr into the last st. Turn.

Work to match back shaping at armhole. At the same time, decrease one stitch on the neck edge until 8[8:10:14] sts remain. Work straight until front matches back.

Work Left Front as per Right Front, reversing all shapings.

## Sleeves

Make two the same. Using the lighter colour, make 27[29:31:33] ch. Starting in the 3rd chain from the hook, work 1dc into each stitch. *26[28:30:32] sts.*

Working the same stitch pattern as for the back and fronts, and keeping the pattern correct, increase 1 st (by working 2 sts into the next st) on each end of the next and every alternate row until there are 38[40:42:44] sts.

Work straight, completing a total of 14 rows in the lighter colour and a further 5 in the darker.

## Shape Sleeve Cap

Keeping pattern correct.
**Row 20:** Work a sl st into each of the next 3[4:5:5] sts, then work 3ch (for the first tr). Work in patt until 2[3:4:4] sts from the end of the row. Turn.
**Row 21:** 3ch (for first tr), dtr2tog, work to last 3 sts, dtr2tog, work 1tr into the last st. Turn.

Repeat this row 3[3:1:2] more times. *28[28:30:30] sts.*

Work 2[3:5:6] rows straight.

**Next row:** 3ch (for first tr), dtr2tog, work to last 3 sts, dtr2tog, work 1tr into the last st. Turn.
Repeat this row twice more.

**Next row:** 3ch (for first tr), dtr2tog, twice, work to last 5 sts, dtr2tog, twice work 1tr into the last st. Turn.
Repeat this row. *16[16:18:18] sts.*

Fasten off yarn.

## Finishing

Block all pieces. Sew shoulders together.
Sew in sleeve caps, easing to fit where necessary.
Sew sleeve and side seams.

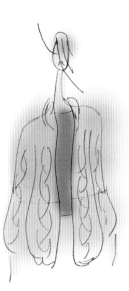

# Cabled Crochet Sweater

Skill Level:
Advanced

Traditional stitches can be used in nontraditional ways. Knitwear from Isabel Marant's Spring/Summer 2012 collection, opposite, incorporates a traditional cable stitch, and the jumper, right, combines the basketweave stitch with cable and bobble panels.

## Cabled Crochet Sweater
Claire Montgomerie

The fashionable knitted Aran-style fabric is copied here utilizing crocheted alternatives to the bobbles and cables of Aran knitting to create a very complex yet extremely satisfying pattern. The style of the sweater is inspired by the 1960s, reminiscent of the beatnik shape, with three-quarter-length sleeves and a wide neckline.

## YARN
11[12:13:15] x 50g (2 oz) balls of JC Rennie chunky lambswool (Aran), 100% wool, 95 m (104 yds), in shade 146, sienna.

## NOTIONS
5 mm (size 6) crochet hook
4.5 mm (size 7) crochet hook
Tapestry needle

## MEASUREMENTS

| XS | S | M | L |
|---|---|---|---|
| **Bust** | | | |
| 76 | 86 | 96 | 106 cm |
| 30 | 34 | 38 | 42 in |
| **Actual Size** | | | |
| 80 | 90 | 100 | 110 cm |
| 31½ | 35½ | 39½ | 43½ in |
| **Length from Shoulder** | | | |
| 52 | 52 | 54 | 56 cm |
| 20½ | 20½ | 21½ | 22 in |
| **Underarm Length** | | | |
| 30 | 30 | 30 | 32 cm |
| 12 | 12 | 12 | 12½ in |

## TENSION/GAUGE
Work 14.5 sts and 12 rows to 10 cm (4 in) over basketweave pattern.

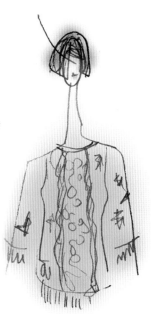

BASKETWEAVE STITCH

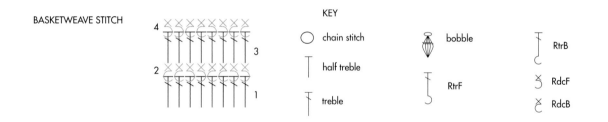

KEY

bobble      RtrB

chain stitch

RtrF      RdcF

half treble

RdcB

treble

CABLE PANEL

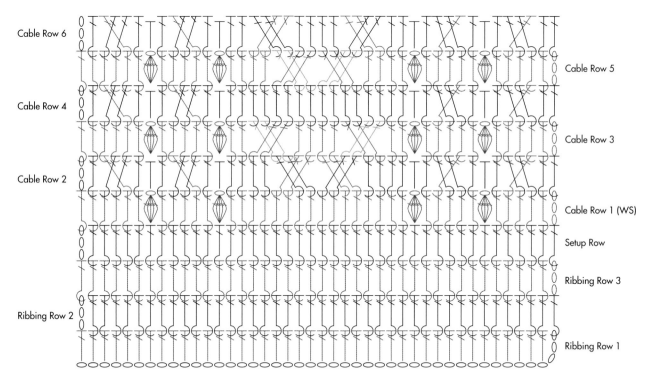

Blue symbols are worked so that they are raised on the RS of the fabric.

Push Bobbles through to RS of fabric.

## SPECIAL INSTRUCTIONS

### Basketweave Stitch

**Row 1(RS):** 1ch (doesn't count as st) (2 RdcF, 2 RdcB) across row.

**Row 2:** 3ch, 1tr into each st across row.

**Row 3:** 1ch, (2 RdcB, 2 RdcF) across row

**Row 4:** 3ch, 1tr into each stitch across row

### Cable Stitches

Front cable panel is worked separately to the rest of front. Back and side panels of front are worked in one piece and then seamed to the cable panel.

Cable panel – beg each section from row one of each pattern stitch when stated in the pattern. Refer to chart opposite for row repeats.

If you have not worked cables before, practise each panel a little prior to working the front. They are not hard to work, just fiddly. The cable does not appear until the second row, so don't worry if it looks messy at first.

**Front Left Cable 4 (FLC4):** Miss 2sts, RtrF in next 2 sts, bring hook in front of sts just made and RtrF in each of 2 missed sts.

**Front Right Cable 4 (FRC4):** Miss 2sts, RtrF in next 2sts bring hook behind sts just made and RtrF in each of 2 missed sts.

**Back Left Cable 4 (BLC4):** Miss 2sts, RtrB in next 2sts, bring hook in front of sts just made and RtrB in each of 2 missed sts.

**Back Right Cable 4 (BRC4):** Miss 2sts, RtrB in next 2sts bring hook behind sts just made and RtrB in each of 2 missed sts.

**Front Left Cable 3 (FLC3):** Miss 1st, RtrF into each of next 2 sts, bring hook in front of sts just made and RtrF in missed st.

**Front Right Cable 3 (FRC3):** Miss 2sts, RtrF into next st, bring hook behind sts just made and RtrF in each of missed sts.

**Make Bobble (MB):** Work 5 incomplete tr into next st – 6 lps on hook – yrh and pull through 5 lps, yrh, pull through rem 2 lps.

### Twist Left (worked over 3 sts)

**Row 1(RS):** FLC3.

**Row 2:** 3 RtrB.

Rep rows 1 and 2 for Twist Left panel.

### Twist Right (worked over 3 sts)

**Row 1(RS):** FRC3.

**Row 2:** 3 RtrB.

Rep rows 1 and 2 for Twist Right panel.

### Lobster Claw (worked over 14 sts)

**Row 1(RS):** RtrB, 2 RtrF, FRC4, FLC4, 2 RtrF, RtrB.

**Row 2:** RtrF, BLC4, 4 RtrB, BRC4, RtrF.

**Row 3:** RtrB, 12 RtrF, RtrB.

**Row 4:** RtrF, 2 RtrB, BLC4, BRC4, 2 RtrB, RtrF.

**Row 5:** RtrB, FRC4, 4 RtrF, FLC4, RtrB.

**Row 6:** RtrF, 12 RtrB, RtrF.

Rep rows 1–6 for lobster claw panel.

### Bobble Panel (worked over 3 sts)

**Row 1(WS):** RtrF, MB, RtrF.

**Row 2:** RtrB, htr into top of bobble, RtrB.

Rep rows 2–3 for bobble panel.

## PATTERN

### Back and Side Panels of Front

Using 4.5 mm (size 7) hook, work 78[94:110:122] ch

**Row 1(WS):** Work 1tr into 4th ch from hook (first 3ch count as 1 tr), work 1tr into each following ch. Turn. *76[92:108:120] tr.*

**Rows 2 and 3:** 3ch, RtrF, (RtrB, RtrF) to end of row.

Change to 5mm hook and cont in basketweave st beg with a row 1 until work measures 33[33:34:35] cm (13[13:13½:13¾] in) in, ending with a row 2.

### Right Front Side Panel

**Next row (RS):** Work in patt over first 7[10:14:16] sts for right front side panel. Place st marker in 5th[7th:8th:9th] st from most recent st; turn, leaving rem sts unworked.

**Next row:** 1ch, sl st in 1st st, patt to end. *6[9:15:16] sts.* Cont in pattern, dec (by 2trtog) one st at armhole edge of every row 2[1:7:10] times more.

Dec at armhole edge of every WS row until 3[2:2:2] sts rem as follows:
**Dec row:** 3ch, tr2tog, 1tr into each st to end. End with a RS row. *6[15:17:18] rows since beg of shaping.*

**S M L Sizes Only:** Work 2 further rows in pattern.
**Next row:** tr2tog. *[18:20:21] rows.*
Fasten off yarn.

**XS Size Only:** Cont in pattern, dec 1 st at both ends of every foll 3rd row until 2 sts rem. Work three rows.
**Next row:** tr2tog. *13 rows.*
Fasten off yarn.

### Back
With RSF, rejoin yarn to back, leaving 4[6:6:8] sts unworked along from right side sts (right armhole).
**Next row (RS):** Work in pattern over next 54[60:68:72] sts for back, place st marker in 5th[7th:8th:9th] st from most recent st. Turn, leaving rem sts unworked.
**Dec row:** 1 ch, sl st in first st, patt to last st, turn, leaving last st unworked. *52[58:66:70] sts.*
Rep last row 2[2:7:10] times more, until 36[36:38:40] sts rem, cont in patt, decreasing as folls on every WS row:

The basketweave, also called the waffle, is a dense, highly textured stitch. In addition to making cosy jumpers, it is a lovely stitch for heavier scarves and blankets.

**Dec row:** 3ch, tr2tog, 1tr into each st to last 3sts, tr2tog, 1 tr. *17[23:24:25] rows since beg of shaping.*

**S M L Sizes Only:** Fasten off yarn.
**XS Size Only:** Continue in pattern, dec 1 st at both ends of every foll 3rd row until 34sts rem.

### Left Front Side Panel
With RSF, rejoin yarn to left front side panel, leaving 4[6:6:8] sts unworked st along from back sts (left armhole).
Work as for right front side panel, reversing all shaping.

### Cable Panel
Using 4.5 mm (size 7) hook ch44.
**Row 1 (WS):** Work 1tr into 4th ch from hook, work 1tr into each following ch. Turn. *42tr.*
**Rows 2 and 3:** 3ch, RtrF, (RtrB, RtrF) to end of row.

Change to 5 mm (size 6) hook and set cable pattern as follows:
**Row 1 (RS):** 3ch, RtrB, (3 RtrF, 3 RtrB) twice, RtrB, 12 RtrF, RtrB, (3 RtrB, 3 RtrF) twice, 2 RtrB. Turn.
**Row 2:** 3ch, RtrF, (3 RtrB, beg bobble panel from row 1) twice, RtrF, 12 RtrB, RtrF, (beg bobble panel from row 1, 3 RtrB) twice, 2 RtrF. Turn.
**Row 3:** 3ch, RtrB, (beg twist right panel from row 1, bobble panel) twice, RtrB, beg lobster claw panel from row 1, RtrB, (bobble panel, beg twist left panel from row 1) twice, 2 RtrB. Turn.
**Row 4:** 3ch, RtrF, (twist left panel, bobble panel) twice, RtrF, lobster claw panel, RtrF, (bobble panel, twist right panel) twice, 2 RtrF.
Rep rows 3 and 4 working the next row of each individual pattern st (see chart).
Continue in this patt until work measures the same length as side panels before shaping, ending with a RS row.

Continue in cable pattern as set, dec1 st at both end of next and every foll WS row until 36[38:38:40] sts rem.
**Next row (RS):** Work across 2sts in pattern. Turn, leaving rem sts unworked.
**Next row:** tr2tog. Fasten off yarn.
Rejoin yarn to opposite edge and work to match.

### Sleeves

Make 2. Using 4.5 mm (size 7) hook, work 34[38:42:42] ch.

**Row 1 (WS):** Work 1tr into 4th ch from hook, work 1tr into each following ch. Turn. *32[36:40:40] tr.*

**Rows 2 and 3:** 3ch, RtrF, (RtrB, RtrF) to end of row. Change to 5 mm (size 6) hook and cont in basketweave st beg with a row 1, increasing 1 st at both ends of row every 6[6:6:6] cm (2½[2½:2:2] in) until there are 40[44:48:48] sts. Cont on these sts until work measures approx 30[30:30:32] cm (12[12:12:12½] in), ending with a WS row.

**Next row (RS):** 1ch, sl st across next 2[3:3:4] sts, work in pattern over next 36[38:42:40] sts. Turn, leaving rem sts unworked. *36[38:42:40] sts.*

**Dec row:** sl st along one st, patt to last st. Turn, leaving rem st unworked. *34[36:40:38] sts.* Rep last row 2[1:7:10] times more.

Continue in patt, until 28[14:10:6] sts rem, decreasing as follows on every WS row:

**Dec row:** 3ch, tr2tog, 1tr into ea st to last 3sts, tr2tog, 1tr.

**S M L Sizes Only:** Fasten off yarn.

**XS Size Only:** Cont in pattern, dec 1 st at both ends of every foll 3rd row until 16sts rem.

### Finishing

Block all pieces lightly.
Set in sleeves using mattress st.
Sew cable panel into front using mattress st.

### Neck

Using 5 mm (size 6) hook, rejoin yarn to any point around neck edge, 3ch and work 90tr evenly around edge, easing in extra sts on smaller sizes by decreasing 4–5 sts across the top of sleeve edge. Join rnd using sl st to top of first ch.

**Next row:** 3ch, RtrF, (RtrB, RtrF) to end of rnd. Sl st to top of first ch to join.

Fasten off yarn and weave in all ends neatly.

## About the Designers

### Irina Antonyuk

www.irenestrange.co.uk

Known for her fun and quirky crochet sculptures and version of the Japanese crochet art of Amigurumi, Irina works as a graphic designer by day and crochets in the evening. Her projects have been published in numerous magazines, such as *Inside Crochet*, *Let's Get Crafting Knit & Crochet* and *Let's Knit* magazine.

### Lesley Arnold Hopkins

Lesley has crocheted since childhood. As a teenager, unable to find patterns that she liked, Lesley began designing her own. She moved away from the delicate antimacassars and mats for dressing tables she'd been taught to make and into more solid fabrics with interesting textures or great colour combinations. A geek at heart, Lesley loves the structure of patterns, the engineering and the maths. Published online and in a number of UK magazines, Lesley is always looking to learn a new technique or find an innovative way of putting stitches together (she rarely makes the same thing twice).

### Zoë Clements

www.love-crochet.com

Zoe was a reluctant lawyer until she discovered a passion for crochet and never looked back. She has been a commissioning editor at *Knit* magazine and a technical editor for *Inside Crochet* and is now a freelance knit/crochet designer, technical editor, writer, teacher and all round yarnophile who runs Love Crochet, an online magazine and resource for patterns, features and tutorials.

### Claire Montgomerie

www.clairemontgomerie.com

Claire is a textiles designer who specialises in knitting and crochet, constructing fabrics, garments, creatures and accessories that are fun, quirky and modern. Her main aim is to reinvent the products of ancient and traditional needlecraft processes, at the same time retaining all of their intricacies and charm. She has made knitwear for film and knitted characters for music videos and animations. Editor of *Inside Crochet* magazine and author of several books, you can find out more about Claire's recent projects and workshops at her website.

### Helda Panagery

www.heldasland.blogspot.com

Helda studied textiles at college and now teaches, writes and designs. She loves creating crocheted fabrics and exploring combinations of yarn texture and stitch pattern. In her work she attempts to keep the shape of garments simple enough to highlight the interesting textures that can be made by hand. Helda is a regular contributor to the UK publication *Inside Crochet* magazine and her designs have also been featured in the *Crochet Calendar*. She runs the London Crochet meet-up, where she teaches and spreads her love of crochet.

## Victoria Stott

With her heart set on a career as a designer-maker and looking for a less-pressured working life, Victoria gave up (almost completely) her teaching career a few years ago. Her inspiration comes from her mother who has always crocheted and gave her lessons when she was very young. She followed in her mum's footsteps quite late in life but is now completely immersed in yarn. Victoria doesn't consider herself to have a "style", as such. She loves to experiment with all kinds of yarn and rarely works from a pattern, preferring to freeform. "I absolutely don't care *what* I am making as long as I'm crocheting something."

## Emma Varnam

http://emmavarnam.co.uk

Art curator and museum manager, Emma learnt how to knit as a child, and throughout adolescence she was at her happiest sewing and making in her spare time. Throughout her twenties she knitted garments for friends and unsuspecting godchildren, but it was only when she had her own son that she started designing. Inspired by the imagination of children, she likes to make garments and toys that evoke a smile. She is particularly drawn to the sculptural quality of crochet, the fact that it can make the most wonderfully intricate patterns and yet be so robust and durable. Emma aims to design beautiful, colourful, practical garments that she would wear herself. She regularly shares her design inspiration and thought processes via her knitting and crochet blog (see above): "My blog is about capturing those little moments of creative magic and taking joy in the small things in life."

## Catherine Wilson

http://getneedled.blogspot.co.uk

Catherine is a crochet and knitting designer and self-confessed yarn addict who loves to experiment with yarn. She has been knitting from the age of six and crocheting since she was 12. She has been designing for Knit on the Net (www.knitonthenet.com) since 2008, and has been credited for her work on Susan Crawford's book *Stitch In Time, Vols I and II*. She has also had designs published in *Inside Crochet* magazine. A full-time student at Edge Hill University and mum of two teenagers, in November 2011 Catherine won a student Creative Arts award for her crochet designs.

## Shops, Emporiums and Suppliers

### UK

**All the Fun of the Fair**
Unit 2.8 Kingly Court
Carnaby Street
London W1B 5PW
Tel: 020 7287 2303
www.allthefunofthefair.bigcartel.com
Quirky haberdashery and yarn store and
website, selling unusual yarns and wools,
embellishments and handcrafted items.

**ArtYarn**
www.artyarn.co.uk
Beautiful wools and fibres, plus hooks,
accessories and crochet patterns.

**Bessie May Yarns**
www.bessiemay.com
Small boutique yarn company supplying
beautiful and unique yarns.

**Coats Craft UK**
Tel: 01484 681881
www.coatscrafts.co.uk
Supplier of yarns and equipment; website
includes list of stockists plus free crochet
patterns and stitch tutorials.

**City Lit, London**
Tel: 020 7831 7831
www.citylit.ac.uk
Runs occasional crochet courses and
workshops.

**The Crochet Chain**
www.thecrochetchain.co.uk
Fabulous shop outside London supplying
all things crochet.

**Crochet Pattern Central** (UK and US)
http://crochetpatterncentral.com
Online directory featuring more than 17,000
links to free crochet patterns and online
tutorials; also good for vintage patterns.

**DMC Creative World Ltd**
Unit 21 Warren Park Way
Enderby, Leicester
LE19 4SA
Tel: 01162 754000
www.dmccreative.co.uk
Supplier of a fabulous range of crochet
yarns, patterns and supplies.

**eBay**
www.ebay.co.uk
Look for sellers of crochet patterns from
the 1930s to the present day.

**Etsy**
http://uk.etsy.com
Handmade online marketplace; search for
crochet yarns, patterns and quirky hooks –
and even sell your pieces.

**Get Knitted**
39 Brislington Hill
Brislington
Bristol BS4 5BE
Tel: 0117 300 5211 (for orders)
www.getknitted.com
Store and online suppliers of wide range of
yarns plus patterns, hooks and books. Store
holds beginners' crochet workshops.

**I Knit London**
106 Lower Marsh
Waterloo, London SE1 7AB
Tel: 020 7261 1338
www.iknit.org.uk
Stockists of wide range of yarns, including
one-off hand-dyed hanks from independent
producers; also hosts crochet workshops
and parties.

**Knit on the net**
www.knitonthenet-shop.com
Online knitting and crochet shop selling
yarns, books and patterns.

**Loop Yarn Shop**
15 Camden Passage
Islington
London N1 8EA
Tel: 020 7288 1160
www.loopknitting.com
Yarn shop and online store for crochet
patterns and haberdashery as well as yarns
from all over the world; also runs classes.

**Makedomenders**
Tel: 01303 813274
http://makedomenders.co.uk
Offers creative craft and crochet
classes and individually tailored
workshops throughout the south east
(established by Claire Mongomerie
and Bee Clinch).

**The Make Lounge**
49-51 Barnsbury Street
London N1 1TP
Tel: 020 7609 0275
www.themakelounge.com
Runs wide range of contemporary craft
workshops and celebratory events such
as hen parties and baby showers from
two purpose-built venues.

**Mrs Moon Yarn & Haberdashery**
41 Crown Road
St Margarets, Twickenham, TW1 3EJ
Tel: 020 8744 1190
www.mrsmoon.co.uk
Stockists of yarns, patterns, books,
hooks and haberdashery; also offers
crochet classes.

**Nest**
102 Weston Park
Crouch End, London N8 9PP
Tel: 020 8340 8852
www.handmadenest.co.uk
Tools and materials for knitting, crocheting,
felting and sewing. Website includes list
of courses.

**Prick Your Finger**
260 Globe Road
London
E20JD
Tel: 020 8981 2560
www.prickyourfinger.com
Textile art collective, online yarn shop
and resource space/gallery.

**Rico Yarns**
www.rico-design.de
An extensive, practical and beautiful yarn
range from this German company.

**Sew-In of Marple, Didsbury and Buxton**
46 Market Street
Marple
Stockport SK6 7AD
Tel: 0161 427 2529

741 Wilmslow Road
Didsbury
Manchester M20 6RN
Tel: 0161 445 5861

1 Spring Gardens
Buxton SK17 6BJ
Tel: 01298 26636

www.myknittingyarnandwool.co.uk
Stocks large range of quality yarns, patterns
and pattern books, needles, hooks and
accessories.

**Yesterknits**
www.yesterknits.com
Largest collection of vintage knitting and
crochet patterns in the world, including
around 50,000 crochet patterns most
published between 1880 and 1980.

## US

**Berroco Yarn**
www.berroco.com
Patterns and yarns are regularly featured
in American magazines.

**Classic Elite Yarns**
Tel: 800 343 0308
www.classiceliteyarns.com
Yarns, patterns (some free), plus list of yarn
stockists.

**Crochet Pattern Central**
http://crochetpatterncentral.com
Online directory featuring more than 17,000
links to free crochet patterns and tutorials.

**Etsy**
www.etsy.com
Handmade online marketplace. Look for
crochet yarns, patterns and quirky hooks –
and sell your pieces.

**Halcyon Yarn**
12 School Street
Bath, ME 04530
Tel: 800 341 0282
www.halcyonyarn.com
Sells extensive selection of yarn and fibers,
books, videos, patterns, and equipment for
knitting, crochet, weaving, and other fiber arts
from store and online, plus workshops.

**ImagiKnit**
3897 18th Street
San Francisco, CA 94114
Tel: 415 621 6642
www.imagiknit.com
Yarn store and website offering yarns and
fibers, news, class schedule, and links to
charity knitting projects.

**Jenkins Woodworking**
www.jenkinswoodworking.com
Beautiful handmade Hairpin Lace looms,
crochet hooks and knitting needles.

**Kaleidoscope Yarns**
www.kyarns.com
Online yarn shop plus crochet patterns,
hooks and books.

**Purl Soho**
459 Broome Street
New York, NY 10013
Tel: 212 420 8796
www.purlsoho.com
Friendly store and online shop selling natural
fiber yarns, needles, books and accessories.

**Ravelry**
www.ravelry.com
Community site, yarn and pattern database
for knitters and crocheters.

**Rosie's Yarn Cellar**
2017 Locust Street
Philadelphia, PA 19103
Tel: 215 977 9276
www.rosiesyarncellar.com
Excellent selection of quality yarns and tools;
also offers knitting and crocheting classes.

**Stitch Diva Studios**
www.stitchdiva.com
Innovative, easy-to-follow knit and crochet
patterns (available by mail, download or at
a yarn store) and yarns at discount prices.
Instructive tutorials, brilliant for learning how to
work Hairpin Lace.

## CANADA

**Karp Styles**
www.karpstyles.ca
Stocks more than 1,000 patterns, plus
crochet hooks and accessories.

**The Knit Café**
1050 Queen St. West
Toronto, Ontario M6J 1H7
Tel: 416 533 5648
www.theknitcafetoronto.com
Stocks natural yarns from all over the world
and offers extensive range of crochet classes.

**Urban Yarns Point Grey**
4437 West 10th Avenue
Vancouver, B.C. V6R 2H8
Tel: 604 228 1122
www.urbanyarns.com
Offers yarns, patterns and accessories from
two stores and website; also crochet classes.

**The Wool Emporium**
12–2605 Broadway Avenue
Avalon Shopping Centre
Saskatoon, SK S7J 0Z5
Tel: 306 374 7848
www.woolemporium.ca
Stocks a variety of quality yarns and offers a
variety of crochet accessories and classes.

# Index

# Acknowledgements

### Author's Acknowledgements

The writing of this book came at a challenging and life-changing period and therefore I would not have been able to complete it without the help of the entire Carlton team, but I must especially extend my gratitude to Lisa, who has been very understanding and supportive.

I must also thank all the wonderfully talented designers who contributed to the book: Irina Antonyuk, Lesley Arnold Hopkins, Zoë Clements, Helda Panagery, Victoria Stott, Emma Varnam and Catherine Wilson. Working with such diverse individuals has been inspiring and enjoyable and it has been a pleasure to see what they produced from the initial inspirations. The same can be said of our wonderfully unique technical editor Charles Voth, who is meticulous and great fun to work with.

Huge thanks must go to the yarn companies who supplied fantastic yarns for the book, especially all at DMC and the lovely and accommodating Helen at Bessie May yarns.

Finally, I must recognize my family, who have been my backbone for the past few months and I would not have got this book finished without their love and support, especially with additional crocheting from my mother, Mary, and help with babysitting from my little sister Gemma. My husband Sean has, as always, provided constant encouragement and sustenance, while there is one little person who has made the whole experience more difficult and more pleasant in equal measure; my baby daughter, Millicent – a distraction that I couldn't be without.